overcoming
fatigue

TRIDENT
REFERENCE PUBLISHING

Published by:
Trident Reference Publishing
801 12th Avenue South, Suite 400
Naples, Fl 34102 USA
Phone: + 1 239 649 7077
Email: sales@trident-international.com
Website: www.trident-international.com

Overcoming Fatigue
© Trident Reference Publishing

Publisher
Simon St. John Bailey

Editor-in-chief
Isabel Toyos

Art Director
Aline Talavera

Photos
© Trident Reference Publishing, © Getty Images,
© Jupiter Images, © Planstock, © J. Alonso

Includes index
ISBN 1582799709 (hc)
UPC 615269997093 (hc)
ISBN 158279958X (pbk)
UPC 615269799581 (pbk)

2005 Edition
Printed in USA

overcoming fatigue

Are you excessively tired?

Getting tired is a natural symptom, which is a result of the process of using energy during the day for a number of daily activities. When you are excessively tired, it's good to take a look at your daily tasks and habits. There are also a number of natural remedies that can help to relieve fatigue.

Feeling tired at the end of the day is natural, and can even be a good feeling because it is an indicator that you need to rest and helps you to go to sleep. However, excessive tiredness tends to appear when you have trouble maintaining healthy habits: not getting regular sleep, not exercising regularly, eating an abnormal or unbalanced diet, smoking, not drinking enough liquids or not dedicating enough time to relax and have fun may cause excessive tiredness.

In order for you to recuperate your normal energy level it is fundamental to know how you could change your daily routine to readapt your lifestyle and incorporate healthy habits. In general, it's good to introduce physical exercise into your daily activities, make sure you stick to a sleep routine, eat a balanced diet, with plenty of nutritious foods that are a good source of energy, and stay away from nervous system depressants, such as alcohol and tobacco. Think about what you could change to achieve a more balanced, stress-free lifestyle.

There are also a number of multi-vitamin

supplements and treatments that are very effective in fighting against tiredness when it is triggered by natural causes or lifestyle habits. In this case it is advisable that you take a higher amount of B complex vitamins (B_1, B_6, B_{12}). Vitamins with antioxidant properties, such as vitamins E and C, can also be effective. Multivitamin supplements contain essential amino-acids (magnesium combined with zinc) and other trace minerals such as magnesium and selenium that help your body recuperate when you are excessively fatigued.

OTHER TIPS
IF YOU FEEL TIRED

It is important that you pay attention to symptoms of prolonged tiredness. This means that even though you have a healthy lifestyle, tiredness persists or increases during a week's time. If you find that you feel fatigued for more than 15 days, it's important that you consult your doctor, because it can be a symptom of an illness. If there is no physical cause for prolonged-fatigue, then it may be advisable to see a psychologist because it might be caused by depression. There is another type of fatigue that is worrisome: this occurs in the evening, after a day of normal, light activities and doesn't disappear after a regular night's sleep. When this occurs, medical attention is recommended.

TO PREVENT GETTING TIRED

To make sure that at the end of the day you aren't excessively tired we've compiled a list of tips so that you can enjoy your leisure time with loved ones:

- Take brief breaks every two hours, especially if your are studying, doing any intellectual task, or working in front of the computer. Stretch out your legs, take a walk and whenever possible, rest your eyes and mind, focusing your attention on the landscape or the view from your room.

- If you work in a closed-in workplace, try to make sure that the space is ventilated so you don't lack oxygen.

- Work in silence or with soft music in the background. Often times, when flooding your sensory perception with information, it is best to avoid the noise of the television and radio or over-stimulating information, while you are working. It is also advised to limit the use of cellular phones.

- Plan out the daily tasks that you need to complete, setting realistic deadlines for the day. This can help you to avoid the tensions that completely exhaust you by the end of the day.

- Eat lunch far away from your workplace and don't take your work with you to lunch . Avoid phone calls and conversations about work during lunch.

- Don't work more than eight hours a day. Reserve private time for yourself and to share with your family and loved ones. This will provide the comfort that you need to fully rest, recharge positive energy and start the next day energized and with enthusiasm.

How to fight fatigue

If simple lifestyle changes and not physical illnesses cause fatigue, there are a number of alternative therapies that can help you to beat tiredness.

You can begin to overcome your tiredness with some simple measures:

■ **Eat well.** Your diet should be balanced and include the principle foods in the food pyramid: lean meats, fruit, vegetables, cereals and low-fat dairy. In addition, it is good to drink 6 to 8 glasses of water a day. Drinking water and fruit juice are important because a lack of liquids and minerals can make you fatigued.

■ **Improve your physical activity.** An exercise routine can be very helpful to help you recuperate your energy. It is recommended to start an exercise program with the supervision of your doctor.

■ **Quit smoking.** Nicotine is a highly addictive drug and cigarettes are very harmful to your health. The effects of tobacco are related to many illnesses that cause fatigue.

■ **Fight insomnia.** Develop techniques and a sleep routine that will help you to rest fully and recuperate from tiredness.

■ **Learn to relax.** There are many techniques, especially with complementary and natural therapies that can help you to relax and revitalize your energy. Developing personal relationships with friends and relatives can be helpful. Also, making time for gratifying activities and having fun is a great way to get over tiredness.

NATURAL ALTERNATIVES

With our stressful, busy lives, most of us experience tiredness sometimes. Daily commutes, overwork, straining physical exercise and changes in lifestyle can be treated, using effective, natural remedies:

- **Herbal medicine.**
  Revitalizing infusions, tinctures and teas.
- **Aromatherapy applications.** Using essential oils on the skin or during massages, or soaking in a hot bath with a few drops of an essential oil (see how to use aromatherapy to revitalize your energy in the list of Essential oils from A to Z, on page 47).
- **Eating energizing foods.** Among the basic foods, complex-carbohydrates found in wholegrain cereals are digested slowly, which permits sugar to be released into the bloodstream slowly. It is also good to eat bananas, apricots and almost all fruits that provide the body with necessary sugars. Beans as soy are a great way to incorporate low-fat protein into the diet (see Foods to fight fatigue, on page 56). However, it's good to consult your medical doctor before starting a new diet; and you should definitely seek medical advice if you suffer from diabetes or if you are overweight.
- **Alternative therapies.** To overcome tiredness there are techniques: yoga, meditation, reflexology, hydrotherapy, energizing Chinese self-massages –do-in and qi gong– (see Complementary therapies, from page 10).

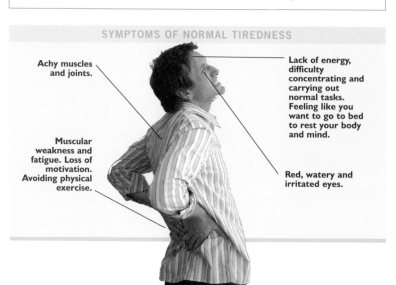

SYMPTOMS OF NORMAL TIREDNESS

Achy muscles and joints.

Muscular weakness and fatigue. Loss of motivation. Avoiding physical exercise.

Lack of energy, difficulty concentrating and carrying out normal tasks. Feeling like you want to go to bed to rest your body and mind.

Red, watery and irritated eyes.

CHANGE YOUR HABITS

If you are busy and constantly on the go, not exercising or taking out the time needed to rest completely can cause excessive tiredness. There are a number of solutions on hand to transform your home and office in sanctuaries for tranquility.

■ At home

There are basic concepts based on the century old Chinese philosophy of *feng shui*, a way to mindfully organize your environment to bring harmony and restfulness into your life:

- Do not place your alarm clock, radios or stereos anywhere near the headboard of your bed or place where you rest. Also, avoid placing computers close to your legs. Electronic equipment have transformers that produce electromagnetic fields that when you are exposed to them over time can cause tiredness.
- Avoid cluttered areas, because they can pollute your vision and the lack of energy flow can affect the nervous system, alternating your vital energy flow.
- Don't combine contrasting colors (for example black and white) in the ceramic tile or flooring in the bathroom or kitchen because the contrast can cause visual fatigue.
- Keep your house dry and ventilated.

■ In your free time

To help you rest up and energize it's good to go out, have fun and get away from your everyday responsibilities. Many entertaining and leisure activities can contribute to being able to rest. In addition, endorphins are released when you are having fun. Endorphins are chemicals produced in

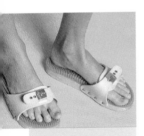

SHOES
You should wear shoes for their utility not because they are in style. Narrow shoes, high heels and uncomfortable designs force the feet into positions that are unstable and unnatural, which not only exhaust your feet but your entire body.

the brain in response to a variety of stimuli, they may be nature's cure for high levels of stress. They lead to feelings of euphoria, moderation of appetite, release of sex hormones and enhancement of the immune responses. Endorphins are released when you exercise, experience orgasms and laugh.

◼ At work

The clothes that you use during the day can also contribute to daily fatigue. To relieve tiredness –and other ailments– it's important to wear comfortable clothes; there is no reason to confuse formal wear with using uncomfortable clothes.

- For women, you should use the size of clothes that are best for your body, don't use tight clothes for fashion's sake. Tight clothes and uncomfortable fabrics can cause a sensation of exhaustion.
- For men, using a necktie too tight, constantly using a suit or using unnecessary jackets can add to tiredness during the day.
- Limit, if possible, the utilization of synthetic fabrics.

Exercise and sports

A regular exercise program can help you to enjoy your body and to avoid tiredness caused by a sedentary lifestyle. It is important to choose physical activity that is appropriate for your age, sex and overall physical fitness, keeping in mind any illnesses or ailments.

✚ Not all physical exercises are the same, some may be better for a particular age group or for your overall fitness. It is recommended to consult your doctor before starting an exercise program to help you choose an activity which avoids overstraining or getting disappointed with your physical level. Studies have shown that regular exercise significantly increases life expectancy and improves overall health. An improved self-image and increased energy level are frequent added benefits of exercise.

Keeping your body in good working condition for daily life and health isn't about running marathons; it's about maintaining a healthy level of physical activity. You can start to exercise at any age, the young and old should incorporate regular physical activity into their everyday lives. Gradually building up the time spent doing the activity by adding a few minutes every few days, when your body feels stronger, faster and more flexible.
Choosing a fitness program can include a

variety of physical activities, from going to a gym, to playing a sport or walking daily. Aerobic activity is good for improving cardiovascular health, losing weight, toning the muscles and increasing your energy level. Aerobic activity is ideal for people who are recuperating from an ailment, who haven't exercised in a while, or for people who are over 50 years of age.

Competitive sports, have the same benefits as aerobic activity, but require time-commitment, a high-level of physical fitness and appropriate training to avoid injuries or other physical risks. It is recommended to begin an exercise program under the supervision of a physical trainer, and only after having a complete physical checkup.

EXERCISING ACCORDING TO YOUR AGE

■ Between 18 and 35 years old

This is one of the best stages in your life to practice sports, because your physical fitness is at its peak. It's ideal to practice sports during childhood because the benefits from physical activity later on in life will be greater. It's recommended to carry out a regular physical fitness routine so that your body stays toned and fit, increasing your stamina so that you don't get tired out as easily. If you exercise or train daily, it's advised to take a break at least one day a week, or to alternate between light exercise and intense physical training, so that your body doesn't get fatigued.

■ Between 35 and 50 years old

If you are in good health, you can do any

DAILY
EXERCISE

Many adults don't realize the amount of exercise that the body needs to stay healthy. It's important to keep in mind the benefits to help continue a regular exercise routine and avoid adapting to a sedentary lifestyle.

However, in order to stay healthy, it is not necessary to exhaust your body doing rigorous exercises. Walking for half an hour or swimming 15 minutes a day is enough to keep our bodies healthy. Other day-to-day tasks such as washing the car, walking up stairs, going for a stroll (with a friend) and cleaning the house are all daily physical activities that keep up our physical stamina.

physical exercise or competitive sport, using precaution. Stamina, flexibility and strength begin to decrease during this age period, increasing the risk of injury and fatigue. It's best to work out at a moderate rate, three days a week. It's also recommended to practice activities that are beneficial for the health but low risk for injuries such as swimming, walking and biking. For those who have practiced sports or worked out regularly throughout life, you can train four to six days per week at a medium-high intensity. It's best to incorporate exercises that increase and support the body's stamina and flexibility, like running for 30 minutes or biking for an hour.

■ Between 50 and 60 years old

Our bodies begin to change: we lose muscle mass, increase fat on the muscles and our capability to recuperate from tired muscles decreases. For this age group it is fundamental to keep active to stay as fit as possible.

Although it would be ideal to practice a competitive sport at this age, it is best advised to go to the gym or to go walking. If up to this age you haven't regularly exercised, it's best to start with a low-impact physical activity and to build up your resistance so that you get less tired. It is recommended to begin sports such as golf, swimming, walking or biking, always after consulting your physician. Symmetric sports are best, that's to say exercises that work out the left side of your muscle mass and the right side too, so that your entire body is equally strong. For those who have played sports or worked out throughout most of their lives, it's best to continue with the favorite sport, okayed by your doctor. However, alternate the sport with some type of gym work out that increases your flexibility like yoga, stretching or pilates.

■ Over 60 years old

Continued and controlled exercise increases the organs' resistance to aging and lowers muscular and cardiovascular deterioration. For those of us in this age group, an exercise routine can help to avoid a sedentary lifestyle and many illnesses.
Recommended sports for this age group include swimming, aqua aerobics and walking.

Yoga for fatigue

Yoga is a technique dating back thousands of years, its philosophical principles and techniques are based on creating harmony between mind, body and spirit. Regularly practicing yoga *asanas* or poses relaxes the body while at the same time revitalizes the lack of energy which causes you to be tired.

✚ Tiredness is a symptom of an imbalance of strength and energy that yoga can help to put back into harmony. While many *asanas* require your body to work hard, over time you will benefit from yoga's relaxing effects: correct breathing, improved oxygen flow in the body, increased energy and better blood circulation.

It's best to practice yoga for 20 minutes, on a padded mat, in the morning before starting your day or in the evening at the end of your day.

It's also advised to begin these exercises with an instructor who can help to familiarize you with the techniques.

GETTING PREPARED

As with all exercises, before practicing yoga postures or *asanas*, you should prepare your body through a series of stretching exercises to warm up your muscles and to release tension.

Rocking chair

This pose is good for loosening and toning your muscles. It is used as a

GENTLE EXERCISE

Yoga is a discipline designed to improve your flexibility and harmony. The exercises use gentle movements without straining your body. When practicing the *asanas* remember not to strain yourself. There is no need to push yourself too far. Remember to use gentle movements and don't push your body into a pose. Throughout time and willpower, you will improve your body's health naturally and get in tune with your body. It is important to remember to use your body with moderation, patience and consistency to prevent side effects like sore muscles or tiredness.

series of movements practiced at the beginning of a yoga session, although it is also good to practice this pose at the end of a session, before meditation. As the name suggests, this *asana* rocks the body, while at the same time increasing your muscle flexibility, releasing tensions, energizing and improving the flow of energy in the spinal cord. It's best to use a moderate rhythm, inhaling through the nose when you move backward and exhaling through the mouth when you move forward.

1. Sit on the floor, with your chin pressed against your chest. Bend your legs, with your feet pressed against the floor. Place your hands behind your knees, with your thumbs pointed outward. Keep your chin pressed to your chest to prevent back injuries.

2. Lift up your feet, supporting them with your arms. Inhale and bring the body backward, maintaining the position of your legs and chin. Rock back and forth five or six times, keeping the legs bent to get the body ready.

3. Once the body has enough elasticity, use the motion to bring the torso backward and to stretch back your legs behind your head. If you can, try to touch the floor with the tips of your toes. Exhale and rock forward, without lifting up your chin. Repeat seven or eight times without stopping. Next, lie back down for a minute or two to relax your body.

BREATHING FOR RELAXATION

Breathing is the body's most important function, which provides the primary element that our bodies need: oxygen. Yoga uses a number of techniques that concentrate on breathing, making yoga ideal for oxygenating, revitalizing and fighting against tiredness.

Nasal breathing –naturally practiced since birth– carries a connection to the cosmic Universe's rhythm. As we grow up and our natural biological processes accelerate, our synchronism with the Universe alters, giving

way to a daily vertigo. When we breathe through our mouths, we absorb more air in less time, but without filling our lungs. Also, when we exhale we don't expel all the carbon dioxide from our lungs.

COSMIC BREATHING

Even though breathing is an instinctive biological function, we tend to breathe incorrectly. The most natural canal for the breath is the nose:

- The tiny hairs inside the nostril filter and purify the air.
- The air is warmed by contact with the veins inside the nostrils.
- It relaxes the nervous system.
- It purifies the body by expelling carbon dioxide.

BREATHING TO RELAX

We have put together a list of exercises that will help you to breathe consciously, to energize you and to revitalize your body, especially when you are tired. However, you should take note that sometimes these exercises can make you dizzy. If this happens, it's best to take a break from the exercises and practice them later with less intensity.

■ Abdominal and Diaphragmatic Breathing

Diaphragmatic breathing uses the diaphragm, a muscle located under our ribs and above our stomach. When we breathe in, we push the muscle down and our stomach moves forward. When we breathe out, the diaphragm moves back to resting position and the abdomen moves back in. It's best to do this breathing technique lying down, on the floor or on a padded mat.

■ Alternate breathing

This exercise consists of inhaling and exhaling through the nostrils alternately. Use your right hand, place your index and middle fingers below your eyebrow and use your thumb to close one nostril at a time, alternating between the right and left nostril.

1. Take a deep breath, inhaling slowly through your nose and expanding your abdomen. Concentrate on your energy in that spot.

2. Slowly exhale, contracting your abdomen before taking another breath. While exhaling, when the air passes through the throat make a sound as if you were snoring. Repeat 4 or 5 complete breaths.

1. Sit with your back straight and your head slightly tilted downward. Begin to exhale through your left nostril, while you close your right nostril with your thumb. Inhale through the same nostril.

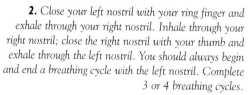

2. Close your left nostril with your ring finger and exhale through your right nostril. Inhale through your right nostril; close the right nostril with your thumb and exhale through the left nostril. You should always begin and end a breathing cycle with the left nostril. Complete 3 or 4 breathing cycles.

POSTURES TO RELIEVE YOUR TENSION

When you are suffering from tiredness, nothing is better to energize the body than yoga. *Asanas* also bring a total state of relaxation.

The Seated forward bend

This *asana* uses slow movements, and is an ideal exercise for moments when you feel exhausted. It brings vitality, literally stretches the back part of the body, at the same time stretches the vertebrae and stimulates blood flow of the back. This pose clears your mind and calms the spirit.

1. Begin by sitting, with your legs together and stretched forward. Keep you back straight and your arms on the sides of your body, supported by your palms. Your body should form a 90 degree angle. Take in a deep breath through the nose and stretch your arms above your head as high as you can, stretching the spine. Do not arch the back.

2. As you exhale bring your chest toward your thighs. Bring your hands to your feet and, if you can, wrap your fingers around them. Breathe comfortably, while you exhale lowering your torso as far as you can. It's ideal to bring your abdomen to your thighs. The idea is to continue right down and hold on to whichever part of your legs or feet you can comfortably reach. You can also place a cord behind your feet and grab onto it instead of your toes.

Reverse pose

This exercise helps the body to recuperate, to clear and calm an exhausted mind and to relieve headaches. It also helps to improve blood circulation especially for the blood flow to the brain.

Begin by lying down with the palms of your hands on the floor, your legs together and looking forward.
Lift up your legs and then your torso. Support your waist with your hands, so that your legs and torso are at an angle. Your feet should be raised directly above your head. Stay in this position for as long as you feel comfortable, breathing slowly. Next, slowly lower the legs and relax your body for a few moments.

Relaxing pose

Although this is a passive pose, this *asana* is beneficial for its ability to relieve tensions and energize the body. Dedicating 10 minutes to this *asana* is equivalent to two hours of deep sleep because of its capacity to recover mental and physical vital energy.

Lie on your back looking for the most comfortable position for your body: shoulders relaxed, back straight, loose hips and legs slightly apart. The tips of your toes should face

outward; your arms, a bit separated from the body, with the palms of your hands open and facing upward. Close your eyes, breathing slowly and deeply. Concentrate on tensing and relaxing each muscle, from your toes to your head. You will feel the weight of your body. Stay in this position for a few minutes, with your eyes closed and without breathing deeply. You will rest significantly in a brief amount of time.

MUDRAS FOR FATIGUE

This technique, dating back thousands of years, uses *mudras* or physical gestures considered sacred for their energetic power to relieve tiredness. Practicing *mudras* is easy and doesn't require a professional practitioner or instructor.

There are four *mudras* or gestures to treat problems of fatigue. You may practice these gestures three times a day for 15 minutes. You can practice *mudras* in any place (except for the dawn *mudra*). Over time and with constant practice you will recuperate lost energy.

■ **Dawn mudra**

1. In the morning, before getting out of bed, clasp your fingers so that your right thumb sits on your left thumb and gently press.

2. Next, bring your hands behind your head and breathe deeply several times, while you open your eyes and mouth. Press your elbows backward against your pillow. You will feel a wave of energy that will help you face the day with more strength.

■ Earth mudra

With your palms facing upward, place the point of your thumbs at the base of your ring fingers. Apply gentle pressure while the rest of the fingers are stretched out. Repeat with both hands. The ring finger symbolizes the earth element, which is stimulated to recuperate strength and physical and mental stamina. You can practice this mudra in the Lotus position or any other position or place.

■ Sky mudra

With your palms facing upward and your thumbs and middle fingers pressed together. Keep the rest of your fingers extended. Practice this mudra with both hands. This gesture stimulates optimism and a good mood. As with the earth mudra, it can be practiced in the Lotus or any other position, without necessarily being an asana.

■ Purifying mudra

With the palm of your left hand facing upward with your thumb, middle, ring and pinkie finger pressed together. Your index finger should be extended, as if you were pointing to something. Repeat on your right hand but this time press your thumb, index, middle and ring fingers together and point with your pinkie. This mudra detoxifies your body and mind. This mudra can be practiced in the Lotus position or any other position.

Restful massages

This series of massages is great to help you relax and to fight stress. They can be done in your own home with the assistance of a relative.

For massages to be truly therapeutic, there are certain guidelines to follow when giving a massage or doing a self-massage. Here are a few tips:

- Pick a quiet and warm room with plenty of light and ventilation.
- The session should be done in silence or with soft music in the background.
- The surface on which the person receiving the massage is lying shouldn't be soft.
- When you are receiving a massage it's good to empty your mind, to help relaxation.

TENSION RELIEVING MASSAGE

This is a series of massages to stimulate blood and lymphatic flow, raising your energy. They help to relieve headaches and sore muscles, in addition to leaving a sense of total well-being. It's recommended to do these massages as a complete series to give truly therapeutic results.

1. Begin with the foot, sliding your thumbs down the foot. This not only relaxes the feet, but the entire body.

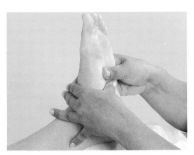

3. Massage the calf muscle to relax tension and to increase blood circulation in the legs.

2. Stimulate the central part of the foot, using pressure in different areas where you accumulate tension. This exercise stimulates blood flow.

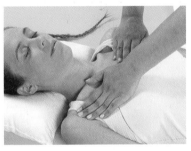

4. Work on the abdomen using circular massages. This massage connects, distends and restores energy in the center of the body.

5. Press your hands gently on the recipient's shoulders to release negative energy in the area near the heart. This pression opens the arteries and activates cardiac rhythm.

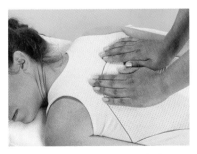

6. Place your hands on the back, the area where we most store tensions. This helps to release blocked energy from the spinal column.

7. Massage the temples to relax better. This movement helps to clear the mind and release worries.

Revitalizing self-massages

This is a series of simple and efficient techniques to give you a "pick-me-up", which will energize and invigorate your body.

➕ This massage can be done at any time of the day you have to take a rest, in private and after taking a hot bath. For this massage to be more effective you should prepare an appropriate atmosphere before giving yourself a self-massage: warm room, soft lighting, and inviting colors. More important than the time you can dedicate to the massage, it's best to choose a moment when you won't be interrupted. The following massages are based on *shiatsu*, an Eastern technique that uses finger pressure on determined points to recover and balance the body's energy.

1. To restore vital energy. Wrap your hand around your foot and keep firm pressure. Gently hit the base of the foot with the edge of the palm of your hand.

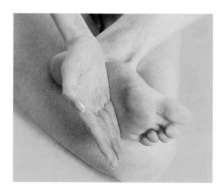

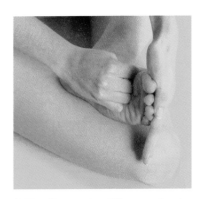

2. *To relieve tension. Wrap your hand around your foot and with the other make a fist and rub your foot with your knuckles, using circular movements.*

3. *To relieve anxiety. Place the thumb of one hand next to the thumb of the other and gently press on the center of the base of the foot. Keep breathing deeply.*

AREAS TO WORK ON TO RELIEVE FATIGUE

On the legs. This point is located the width of your hand below your inner knee joint, in the hollow point between the femur and the muscle. Press on this point on both legs to relieve pains, especially from the waist down.

On the shoulders. Lift up your arm and look for the hollow place below the shoulder muscle. Once you've located the point apply pressure with your index fingers and thumbs; lower your arm and begin to massage by applying even pressure. Repeat on your other shoulder.

On the wrists. This point is found on the inner part of each of the wrists. Rub with your thumbs. Press on each wrist to relieve physical fatigue. This technique helps to relieve intense exhaustion.

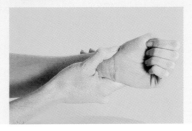

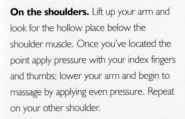

Qi gong energy exercise

Qi gong self-massage originates in Chinese medicine, it is a series of techniques for stimulating and balancing the flow of *chi* energy with soft movements that harmonize the body's functions.

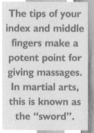

✚ During the practice of *qi gong*, the hands are transmitters and receptors of energy. The technique trains the hands to become sensitive and efficient in detecting energy channels and the *laogong* point and a key tool called the Sword.

> The center of the palm of your hand is where the *laogong* is found, where a number of meridian channels meet. When you are giving a *qi gong* massage or self-massage, keep in mind that this point is a radar for detecting blocks, energy sources and deficiencies.

When beginning *qi gong* massages it is important to clear your mind and concentrate on your hands and the part you are massaging. For more stimulating effects, repeat the massages between 15 and 30 times or for 10 minutes.

> The tips of your index and middle fingers make a potent point for giving massages. In martial arts, this is known as the "sword".

■ **Friction on the hands.** *Before beginning a qi gong session and between massages it is important to rub the palms of your hands together. During this technique you should concentrate on the laogong point and the points on the fingers.*

REACTIVATING THE CHI

To use the *qi gong* self-massages, stand up with your body relaxed and your feet about shoulder width apart. This technique will activate your vital energy.

■ **On the forehead.** *Massage your forehead with one hand and then the other, rubbing from one temple to the other. This technique activates the nervous system and the blood flow in this sensitive area of the head.*

■ **On the scalp.** *Place your fingertips on your scalp, on the sides of your head. Rub forward and then backward. Next, apply pressure with your nails, as if they were a comb and use friction in the same way. This massage helps to stimulate your vital energy and fight against fatigue.*

■ **On the eyes.** *Cup your hands. Place your index and your pinkie over your eye sockets, while your other two fingers touch your eyelids lightly. The massage consists of an energetic friction from the eyes to the temples. This helps your eyes take a rest.*

■ **On the face.** *Place your hands in front of your face. Rub down, starting with your forehead, in front of your eyes, until your chin. Separate your hands and apply friction, moving upward. This technique invigorates the energy in the face, tones the skin and facial muscles, preventing premature wrinkles.*

■ **On the ming men.** This center is an important place in the body, where our vital energy is stored. It is located between the second and third lumbar vertebrae, just beneath the two kidneys.

This self-massage is practiced in two steps, benefitting the flow of energy through the meridians and harmonizing the function of the kidneys. Make a fist, making sure that your thumb sits on your index finger, forming a circle. Keep your wrist lose. This posture is called the Tiger's mouth.

1. With your fists rub the ming men point, using circular motions, 15 times clock-wise and 15 times counter clock-wise.

2. Next, with your fists gently tap on the ming men points, alternating between the right and left hand side.

■ **On the arms.** This massage is used to activate the flow of the *chi* (vital energy) through the meridian acupuncture points in the arms.

1. With your left hand open, massage the right arm, first on the inside of the arm to the shoulder with your fingertips.

2. Next, massage up the outer arm until you reach the shoulder. Repeat 15 times and change arms.

■ **On the dantian.** The *dantian* refers to the central point in the lower abdomen, three fingers beneath the navel where the vital energy is refined and converted into subtle energy for distribution to the rest of the organism. This massage will make you feel as if you have heat running through the abdominal cavity. This self-massage is practiced in two stages.

1. First, place your hands over the point and diagonally rub 30 times, with one hand moving upward and the other downward.

2. Next, place your hands in the "tiger's mouth" position and gently tap on the dantian 30 times, to distribute energy.

■ **On the arms.** This technique stimulates the circulation of the *chi* through the meridians in the legs. The same friction technique is used on the arms and the legs.

With the palms of your hands massage the outer thigh, until your ankle. Next, massage up the inner part of the legs, until the thigh and then massage downward. Repeat 30 times.

AN ENERGIZING EXERCISE

This massage helps when you are exhausted, improves concentration and relieves headaches.

1. Begin standing with your legs parallel shoulder width apart and your knees slightly bent. Your arms should stay at the sides of your body; your shoulders relaxed.
2. Lift up you arms, straighten with the palms facing upward, to the height of your shoulders. Whilst, breathing deeply, direct the breath toward the *dantian*, as if gathering the energy that is generated from there.
3. Next, inhale and bend your forearms placing your hands on your shoulders. Exhale while you release from this position.

Resting your feet

Reflexology is a natural healing art based on the study and practice of the principle that there are reflexes in the body –especially on the hands and feet– that correspond to the body's organs and glands. Applying stimulation and pressure to the feet or hands has a similar effect to a total body massage.

✚ Daily activity and excessive physical work over short periods of time can exhaust your body, bringing on bouts of fatigue. Reflexology or reflexotherapy releases blocked energy and helps it flow. There are connections between different parts of the body. Reflexology is not an exact science, but is considered a natural healing art.

Reflexology has been used since around 3,000 B.C. particularly in China, but also in Malaysia and India. However, archeologists have found paintings referring to this technique in the Egyptian pyramids. Modern reflexology is based on the work of US physician William H. Fitzgerald, who in the early 20th century developed the ancient Oriental healing art of using pressure to relieve pains into a usable diagnostic therapy. Fitzgerald's nurses aid, Eunice Ingham, further pioneered a reflexology foot chart, which we use as a guide today and have included on this page.

FOOT REFLEXOLOGY

There are a number of reflexology zones on the body, including the hands and ears. However, the foot is the area with most concentrated energy pathways and the easiest and most effective technique to practice. We've put together a beginners guide to foot reflexology. The essential points to treat tiredness are drawn in the diagram:

- On both feet: the areas representing the neck, shoulders, waist, spinal column, sacrum, coccyx, solar plexus, head and heart.
- On the outer part of the feet: lower back, knee, leg and back.
- On the inner part of the foot: the sacral, lumbar, thoracic and cervical areas. And on the instep, the hip.

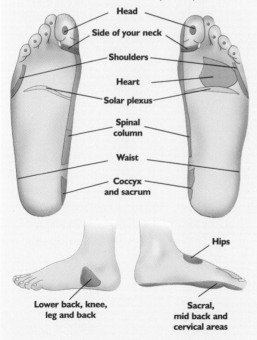

Head
Side of your neck
Shoulders
Heart
Solar plexus
Spinal column
Waist
Coccyx and sacrum

Hips

Lower back, knee, leg and back

Sacral, mid back and cervical areas

STIMULATING DETAILS

- For tiredness a reflexology massage can be used to revitalize you at any time. However, the best time of the day to practice reflexology is in the morning because it prepares your body to start the day and to face everyday stress and taxing tasks. It can also be good to practice in the afternoon to decongest and relieve tension.
- It's always best to use high quality essential oils and foot creams.
- You can light incense sticks and put on soft music: taking care where you apply reflexology is a good way to improve results.
- Don't forget to take time for a foot massage for the health of the entire body.

FOR PERSONAL RELAXATION

Reflexology, is based on the study of meridians that run throughout the whole body. Although an experienced practitioner should apply reflexology, there are massages based on this technique that you can do yourself to relieve discomfort. There are a number of techniques to treat tiredness, which activate lost or blocked vital energy.

Getting ready

Before giving yourself a reflexology massage, it's recommended to sit in a comfortable position so that you can reach your feet. Do not bend your back, because you will block the flow of your breath. Although you can give yourself a massage with your socks on, it's best to do these exercises in your bare feet. Begin with a relaxing manual technique: wrap your hand around your ankle and roll your foot with your other hand.

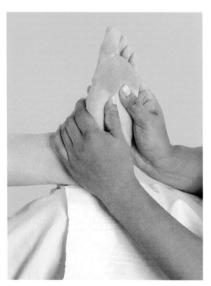

Self-massages that relieve

After getting ready and following the diagram with the reflex points in the feet (see *Foot Reflexology* box, on page 31), you can begin with the following exercises when you feel tired and to give you a pick-me-up.

1. Begin by applying pressure to the central point in the left foot to release built up tension. This point corresponds to the heart, an area where excess tension tends to be stored.

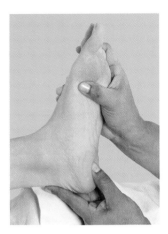

3. Activate the side of the foot, the area that corresponds to the upper back. With your other thumb, press on the heel to massage the coccyx. This allows you to open the energy flow in the vertebrae.

2. Press on the point that corresponds to the spinal column. One finger placed on the upper part of the foot to work the cervical bones and the other on the lower part of the foot to work the back. This massage is especially good for tense muscles caused by straining activity.

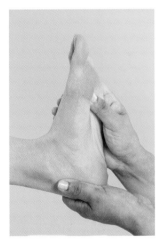

4. With your thumb, press on the reflex point for the chest cavity on the opposite foot. This movement promotes balance and harmony in the body and gives a sense of over-all well-being. You may feel like yawning or sighing after experiencing this relaxation technique.

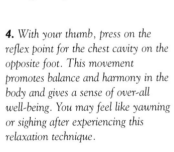

PAY ATTENTION TO YOUR BODY

Because tiredness can cause a number of symptoms, it is important to consider the messages the entire body sends to relieve the aches and ailments caused by exhaustion. Locate the reflex points in the feet that correspond to sore or tired parts of your body and apply pressure. The most effective and relaxing points tend to be the chest cavity, head, heart, shoulders and any other muscle or organ that is achy.

Color to make you feel better

Color therapy is a set of principles used to create harmonious color for healing. According to the principles of this therapy, color is energy. This form of energy medicine is based on the belief that the human body is composed of energy fields. This therapy stimulates the nerve centers and works on problems related to energy deficiencies which may cause physical and mental exhaustion.

✚ Well before science recognized the medical benefits of the ultraviolet and infrared wavelengths, natural healers used color therapy in treatment of patients. Greek philosopher Hippocrates said: *Human beings should harmonize the body and spirit.*
Today, natural medicine and color therapy are based on properly distributing energy.

COLOR AS TREATMENT

A typical color therapy session is done in a dark room, with colored optical slides, cromotherapy lamps or a simple slide projector. Colored light might be applied to parts of the recipient's body or to his entire body. The person recieving this therapy should be relaxed and focused on the color applied. The lights may be used constantly or rhythmically. The technique of solarized water is a simple and cheap way of applying color to the body. Water, when exposed to sunlight in a colored container for at least an hour becomes irradiated and takes on some of the vibrational energy of that particular color. Using this same method you can also prepare solarized sugar or oil.

The power of colors

All colors, depending on their characteristics have curing powers, and each color is applied for varying ailments.

Red. Activates the circulatory system. Stimulates the process of learning and concentration; increases your will power and constancy.
• Ideal for fighting against weariness in the body, especially when you are experiencing tiredness in general. It is recommended to incorporate red into a room used for study for ideal concentration and creativity. It is also recommended if you need to study, write, read or do any intellectual task and feel tired.

FOR EACH *CHAKRA*, A COLOR

Oriental disciplines have for centuries considered *chakras* centers of energy. Each *chakra* corresponds to a certain color of lights applied to that point to balance the body's natural energy.
• *Chakra* on the crown of the head: **violet.**
• *Chakra* of the third eye, in the center of the forehead: **indigo.**
• *Chakra* of the throat: **turquoise, blue** and **sky blue.**
• *Chakra* of the heart: **green.**
• *Chakra* of the chest cavity: **yellow.**
• *Chakra* of the suprarenal glands: **red.**
• *Chakra* of the reproductive organs: **orange.**

Orange. Useful for nervous exhaustion. Lifts up the spirit and leaves a sense of euphoria.

• If you lead a sedentary life, incorporating this color into your surroundings can stimulate your willpower, lift you up and make you want to get up and move around.

Yellow. Relaxes the muscles and reduces excess worry when you are under pressure.

• Helps in situations when you are pessimistic or unsatisfied. Using yellow clothing during the day can lift up your energy and sleeping in a yellow room will help you to wake up in the morning.

Green. Regenerates the body's cells, relaxes the muscles and relieves tired sight. Soothes tensions and aggressions and renews optimism.

• This pain relieving color can be used to calm aches and pains. This is an ideal color for a room you use for rest.

Blue. This color gives a sense of relaxation and restfulness. Helps to get over fears.

• A massage under blue light can help to relieve pain and gives immediate results. Helps you to recover from tiredness and makes other therapies like massages more effective.

Violet. Detoxifies the body, supporting the expulsion of toxins and improving oxygen flow to the cells. Stimulates brain activity.

• Stimulates blood flow to the brain, activating intuition and inspiration. This color is the perfect color in the place where you must work hard and use brain power, because it reduces stress and tension.

White. Fortifies the immune system. Produces a state of positive energy and good spirits.
Enlivens and empowers other color rays. It is the best color for inside your house to maintain a calm spirit and a constant energy.

RECIPE FOR CHARGED WATER

Place mineral water or spring water in a bottle of the color which you need, or improvise with a clear bottle covered with colored cellophane. Expose the water to sunlight from the morning until dusk and then store in a dark place. Water is used to treat different problems. It can be taken in a dose of 3 tablespoons a day, preferably before meals or during fasts. Children can take up to 2 spoonfuls a day.

INCORPORATE COLOR IN YOUR LIFE

Knowing the properties of color you can use them in your daily life to activate your vital energy when you are tired. Using colors depends on your creativity and personal taste. Some alternatives for using colors include:

- Decorative paintwork on the walls of your home.
- Clothes and accessories.
- Filtered lamps that reflect different tones.
- Objects or adornments with stones or colored crystals.
- Choosing foods for their colors.

- Paintings of landscapes –or landscapes to visit– where certain colors predominate.

Water, flowing with energy

Since ancient times water has been used as a natural medicine to cure the human body. Hydrotherapy is the use of water at different temperatures to revitalize, maintain, and restore health. There are a number of hydrotherapy techniques that use cold or hot water to stimulate the nervous system and to soothe pain.

✚ Water is considered by Chinese medicine to be one of the five basic elements that carry curative properties for the body and the soul. Ancient cultures in the East and West have used water for its curative properties: the bath has been used as a ritual to eliminate impurities in almost all religions.

HYDROTHERAPY TO FIGHT FATIGUE

Taking a cold or hot water bath with essential oils or herbs provides incredible therapeutic effects. Other techniques include soaking, washing, rubbing and compresses.

WARNING

You should always consult your physician before starting any alternative treatment. If you suffer from high blood pressure, you should not use cold water.

Bath

Depending on your energy level and physical state there are different water temperatures you can use.

■ **Cold water.** Increases your sensitivity, shrinks your blood vessels, stimulates your blood pressure and tones the nervous system.

■ **Warm or hot water.** Relaxes tense muscles and supports the immune system.

If you take a shower its best to:
- If it is cold, remain under the water for five minutes.
- If the water is hot or warm, stay in the shower for fifteen minutes.

If you are soaking in a bath, it's recommended:
- If you use warm water to restore your energy and improve circulation, stay in the water for five minutes and then exercise so that you warm up or rest in a warm bed.
- If you use warm water to relax and to relieve achy muscles, stay in the water for ten minutes.
- You can also add the bath salts or essential oils recommended for resting to the bath (see *Essential oils from A to Z*, on page 47).

Warning. It's advisable to avoid these types of baths if you suffer from low blood pressure.

> **FOOT BATH**
> This is an ideal therapy to relieve tired feet and legs. You should fill a bucket with cold water, high enough so that you soak your legs. As with baths, you can add essential oils to the water to help you rest. Soak your feet and legs for a minute. Remove your legs from the water, dry off and cover your feet with cotton socks and rest for a while.

SPRAY SHOWERS

This is a type of massage using shower jets to apply pressure. It helps to tone the muscles, stimulate oxygen flow to the muscle tissues, increases the skin's resistance, stimulates circulation and, more than anything, helps to rejuvenate your body.

•**On the face.** This is a relaxing technique for the body and mind and it is perfect for treating headaches and migraines. Begin with the forehead, placing it under cold water and moving the water round in a clock-wise direction. Don't stop breathing, breathe through your mouth.

• **On the arms.** This is a shower technique that will give you an instant pick-me-up, because it activates circulation and stimulates deep breathing.

I. Begin by passing the cold waterjet on your right hand along the outter part of the right arm and move up until your shoulder, leaving it under the water for a few minutes.

2. Next, run the inner part of you arm under cold water, from your triceps to the palm of your hand. Repeat on the left side.

For cases of tiredness and lack of concentration, use this shower therapy on your arms, alternating between warm and cold water.

Relieving aromas

Aromatherapy uses essential oils extracted from herbs and plants as a technique to care for the body. Essential oils can be used for their aromas and can be applied to soften the skin and penetrate the skin pores. This therapy restores the nervous system and leaves one in a highly relaxing state.

✚ Essential oils can be used in order to balance physical, psychological and spiritual symptoms. Their aromas affect the sense of smell while smoothly penetrating through your skin and revitalizing your nervous system. Essential oils can be added to baths, salves and used in massages to relieve tiredness and other ailments. We have put together a list of *Essential oils from A to Z*, on page 47. Following the list are several recipes for home treatments against fatigue.

ANGELICA TO CLEAR THE MIND

Wherever you study, read or meditate prepare an aromatherapy clay pot with 3-5 drops of angelica essential oil to improve your concentration. This oil can be even more potent when mixed with patchouli.

INVIGORATING BATH

Add 10 drops of angelica oil to a warm bath and soak away. This aroma gives a sense of confidence and balances the mind. It is recommended to use this therapy when you have to make an important decision.

JUNIPER

Sleepy bath: dilute 10 drops of this essential oil to a filled bath tub. After soaking you will feel calm and relief from tensions and tiredness.

RESTFUL BATHS
Dilute 10 drops of essential oil of juniper to a bathtub. In addition, add 3 or 4 drops of essential oil of mandarin or camomile, to help you recover from sleepiness or mental exhaustion.

ANTI-DEPRESSIVE AROMATHERAPY

Place an opened bottle of juniper oil close to your face and leave it there for a few minutes while you continue breathing normally to absorb the aroma. Next, place the bottle close to the solar plexus, continuing to breathe. Immediately you will feel energized and your mood will improve.

EUCALYPTUS TO CLEAN YOUR BODY AND YOUR HOME

This essential oil can be used to relax or purify spaces where you've had arguments or experienced stress. Prepare a spray bottle with 10 drops of eucalyptus oil and 2 cups of spring water. Spray the room and your face with this aromatic water.

GINGER CALMING MASSAGES

Essential oil of ginger is very effective to relieve tension when used in massages. This oil has very potent properties that stimulate the blood flow. It should always be diluted because it can irritate the skin. Its sedative effect can calm sore muscles caused by fatigue; to treat achy muscles massage a few drops directly onto the sore area.

LIMONCELLO OR LEMON HERB TO REST AT NIGHT

At night, dilute 4 drops of lemon oil in an aromatherapy clay pot, to recover from an exhausting day and to help relax and enjoy evening activities like reading.

LEMON TO IMPROVE STUDY

Dilute a few drops of lemon oil in a spray bottle
with a small amount of water
and spray the room where
you are going to read
or study. This aroma can
improve your concentration.

ROMAN CAMOMILE RESTFUL BALM

Dilute a few drops of camomile
with a bit of water and moisten linen cloths to
use as compresses for sore or fatigued muscles.

RELAXING BATH
Add a few drops
of camomile oil to
a warm bath,
soaking in this
fragranced water
will help you get
away from your
worries and rest.

FOR YOUR FEET
Apply pressure to
reflexology points
on your feet, using
essential oil of
camomile. This
will relax and calm
your spirit, helping
to change
your mood.

RELAXING MASSAGES

*Add a few drops of essential oil of camomile in a
small bottle with sweet almond oil and use for back
and abdominal massages. This therapy is great for
when you are feeling oversensitive; this oil is ideal for
fighting against insomnia and anxiety.*

NIAULI PURIFING

This oil is useful if you work at home. It's advised to "purify" the energy that charges the room, which can interfere with rest. Dilute a few drops of niauli oil in a spray bottle with water and spray the room. This essence lifts up your spirits and energizes. Because it's a strong fragrance, you may want to mix a few drops of geranium oil, which stimulates positive thinking.

PINE VAPORS TO FIGHT FATIGUE

Add 7 drops of pine essence to 2 cups of hot water. Put a towel over your head and tilt your head over the bowel and inhale for 15 minutes.

Warning. Before using this oil it's best to test your sensitivity, applying a small amount on your skin and leaving it for 15 minutes to make sure it doesn't irritate your skin or cause an allergic reaction.

ESSENCE
BLENDS

**Formulas
to pick you up**

Use a clay pot in a room you can relax in after a strenuous day at work. Here are two of the most efficient formulas:

- 3 drops of lemon,
  3 drops of orange,
  4 drops of bergamot.
- 3 drops of lavender,
  4 drops of cedar,
  3 drops of orange.

ACTIVE MEDITATION

Fresh pine makes us think of the mountains. Add a few drops to a clay pot for aromatherapy; sit or lie down in a comfortable position, close your eyes and visualize a forest. This essence evokes a sense of peace and erases daily exhaustion.

WARNING

Aromatherapy clay pots shouldn't be used for more than two hours, because prolonged exposure to fragrance can cause headaches or neutralize the therapeutic effect of each essential oil.

ROSEMARY MOTIVATING BATH

This herb has gently euphoric properties, indicated in cases of psychological problems for those who feel disappointed or unable to achieve their objectives. Add a cup of rosemary infusion to a warm bath. You will feel energized and optimistic.

VIGORIZING CLARY SAGE

Draw up a warm bath, add a few drops of clary sage essence and soak in the bath no longer than 15 minutes.
Clary sage produces a sense of euphoria and calms anxiety. Because this bath therapy can make it difficult to concentrate, you shouldn't drive afterward. It's best to use clary sage before going to bed, because it can induce sleep.

REVITALIZING CLARY SAGE
Add a few drops of sage essential oil to a warm bath. This oil can be used for cases of extreme exhaustion, when the body feels fatigued and sore. In Chinese medicine this herb is known as a *yin* tonic, because it calms and at the same time stimulates the nervous system.

Herbs and essentials to relax

Medicinal herbs can be taken as infusions or capsules to fight tiredness. While essential oils, also made from herbs can be used in aromatherapy. In the following pages, we have developed a guide of the most efficient plants that work as remedies for tiredness and a list of essential oils from A to Z, that when used externally can help fight fatigue.

TONIC INFUSION
Place 2 teaspoons of dried echinacea in 1 cup with boiling water. Let steep for 5 minutes, drain and drink.

NOTE
You should always consult your physician before starting any herbal treatment.

Echinacea
(Echinacea purpurea and Echinacea angustifolia)

• **Parts used.** The root and flowers are used. Powdered echinacea and tincture are made from the plant's roots. Relatively recently, the flowers began to be used to make capsules.

• Echinacea is a wild flower native to North America. Native Americans used the plant for a variety of conditions, including high fevers and venomous bites.

• This is one of the most widely used natural remedies in the West, because of its antiviral and antibacterial properties. It supports and stimulates the body's immune system.

• It is not known what causes echinacea's curative actions, but it can be used in cases of fatigue for its stimulating-tonic properties.

Ginkgo Biloba
(Ginkgo biloba)

• **Parts used.** The seeds and leaves are used in homemade infusions, which haven't been proven effective. However, it has been demonstrated that ginkgo extracts and capsules made from the plant's leaves are very effective.

You can find them in health food stores.
• The ginkgo tree species is native to China. During the Middle Ages, it was believed by Europeans that this tree came from the Garden of Eden.
• It is a powerful tonic for the mind. Ginkgo extract activates the metabolism of the brain, improving blood and oxygen circulation.
• Its active properties improve memory, lack of concentration, depression and other ailments related to fatigue.
• **Warning.** Although this plant doesn't have serious side effects, the seeds can be toxic. It's not recommended for children or the elderly to take this remedy. You shouldn't use the seeds, because their extract can be irritating.

RINGING IN YOUR EARS
This persistent and bothersome symptom can be caused by insufficient circulation in the brain. This ailment can cause headaches, exhaustion and fatigue. Take 80 to 120 mg of ginkgo extract capsules a day, always under medical supervision.

ESSENTIAL OILS FROM A TO Z

ANGELICA
Stimulates the nervous system, relieves fatigue and improves concentration. Use in baths, vapors, massages and compresses. It blends well with clary sage and lemon.
Safety. Excessive use can have a narcotic effect and decrease blood circulation. Can be toxic in high doses. It increases your photo-sensibility, making it important to avoid direct sunlight after using.

CLARY SAGE
This potent sedative can be used in vapors.
It releases tensions that prevent the free flow of energy. It also calms the nerves and clears the mind. As it helps to awaken contemplation, it is good for meditation.
Safety. It should be used in low doses, because it can be soporific.

WARNING
Essential oils are for external use **only**, they should **never** be ingested. Keep stored away from children and keep away from your eyes.

FOR MORE ENERGY
It's recommended to take 1-2 tablets of Siberian ginseng once a day, always under medical supervision.

ENERGETIC TONIC
For a lasting effect, prepare a decoction with guarana seed. Prepare by adding 2 teaspoons of crushed guarana seeds to 1 cup of boiling water and let steep for 5 minutes. Drain and drink 2 or 3 cups a day.

Siberian ginseng
(*Eleutheroccoccus senticosus*)

• **Parts used.** The roots. Fresh or dried Siberian ginseng root is not available on the market, you can only buy it in capsule form, made from a base of the root.

• Stimulating effects that increase physical and mental stamina, especially for cases of extreme exhaustion.

• There are three varieties of this plant, but when it is used in Chinese medicine it is used in particular for cases of energy deficiency, or lack of vital energy in the heart. It also has physical therapeutic effects, calming heart palpitations, supporting the immune system and assisting the body in tolerating aggressions.

• **Warning.** Do not take ginseng continuously for more than four weeks. It can cause insomnia and high blood pressure. It's best to avoid coffee or caffeinated tea while using ginseng. You should not take this remedy if you are healthy, only take it if you have signs of tiredness or physical fatigue. This remedy is not recommended for pregnant women or for children under 12 years old.

Guarana
(*Paulina cupana*)

• **Parts used.** The seeds, covered in a shell are toasted and ground to make a brown powder. The roots are also used.

• This plant native to the Amazon area, produces a seed rich in caffeine and other stimulating substances. The indigenous people of the Amazon rain forest use crushed guarana seed as a beverage and a medicine.

• Stimulates the central nervous system and promotes the release of adrenaline. Keeps your

arteries clear, elastic, supporting good blood circulation in the body.

• Thanks to its caffeine content, it prolongs stamina and increases the body's capacity to use physical strength.

• It promotes the use of glucose in the muscles, benefiting the muscular tissue, increasing the muscle's stamina against fatigue. Used as a tonic and general stimulant, it fights against physical exhaustion, fatigue or low energy.

• Can be used in tablets (made with the dried extract) or in a powder to mix with juices and other liquids.

• It shouldn't be used with other stimulants (ginseng, coffee, maté, etc) or with tranquilizers.

• **Warning.** Avoid guarana if you suffer from caffeine intolerance, high blood pressure, serious cardiovascular disorders, ulcer and insomia. It shouldn't be taken during pregnancy and lactation. Avoid giving children guarana.

A REMEDY FROM THE AMAZON

In the Amazon forest guarana is traditionally prepared by toasting the seeds to avoid fermentation. Natives use a traditional method of preparation by drying and roasting the seeds and mixing them with water to make a paste. The mixture is cooked over fire. This is called "guarana paste", which the indigenous people drink by placing it in a cup of hot water throughout the day as an energetic tonic.

ESSENTIAL OILS FROM A TO Z

EUCALYPTUS

Its aroma stimulates and clears the mind; strengthens the nervous system and immune function, increasing your body's defenses when you are tired or fighting an illness. It purifies the air and body. This potent aroma can be used in sprays, baths, compresses or massages; when using on the skin eucalyptus should be diluted.

Safety. Can irritate the skin. Shouldn't be used if you suffer from high blood pressure.

GINGER

Intense stimulant that at the same time comforts and brings on a sense of euphoria, which can help to relieve states of extreme tiredness. This nervous tonic calms your emotions and improves your memory. It also has revitalizing effects, especially when used with other oils like ylang ylang, lavender and angelica. It can be added to baths, vapors, massages and compresses.

Safety. If you have sensitive skin, it is advised to use this oil diluted.

Huang qi
(*Astragalus membranaceus*)

• **Parts used.** The roots are extracted from the plant when it is 4 to 7 years old; the roots are cultivated in the spring. It is used to prepare infusions, make capsules or tinctures, which can be found in most natural food stores.

• *Huan qi* in extracts strengthens the body's inmune system and increases the production of antibodies to fight off external cell destruction and tumor cells.

• *Chi* or essential energy tones the body. It is also called the factor of resistance because in Chinese medicine it is prescribed for cases of fatigue or weakness.

• There are three ways to take *huang qi*: decoction of fresh or dried root; in capsules or tablets made from dried extract of the plant; in tincture (made with alcohol maceration).

• **Warning.** Do not take with other stimulants, like gingseng, coffee, tea or maté.

Recommended dose:

• Take 3 to 5 teaspoons of fresh root per day in a decoction.

• Supplements usually contain 500 mg of *huang qi*. Take 2 or 3 capsules per day.

• Tincture, take 1 teaspoon 3 times a day.

Pink trumpet tree
(*Tabebuia avellanedae*)

• **Parts used.** The internal bark that is

FIGHTING TIREDNESS

Prepare a decoction of the bark, placing 1 tablespoon of the bark in 2 cups of cold water and let boil 5 to 15 minutes. Filter and drink throughout the day.

JUNIPER

Its stimulant properties clear and tone the mind. Especially good if you are under a lot of pressure or with a lot of responsibilities, if you feel tired or if you feel anxious or antsy. Excellent antidepressant, this oil develops the spirit's harmony; its fresh aroma lifts up your spirits and improves your self-esteem. It blends well with geranium, lavender and vetiver.

Safety. Shouldn't be used during pregnancy, because excessive use can bring on birth. High doses and concentrates can irritate the skin.

LEMON

Used to treat psychological symptoms of tiredness because it clears and refreshes the mind, increasing concentration, improving energy and emotional well-being. Blend with incense, ylang ylang or camomile.

Safety. This essence can irritate the skin if it isn't diluted. Because of its photo-toxic effects it's best to avoid exposure to sunlight after using it.

collected from wild trees, to prepare in decoctions, medicinal tinctures and salves.

• This tree, native to South America, is valued for its hard wood and its curative properties for treating complex ailments like post-viral fatigue, recuperating from an illness, loss of energy and fighting cancer with coadjutant treatments.

• Many of its components stop the growth of tumors, by impeding their metabolism of oxygen.

• Because of its properties it is used to restore a body tired out by fatigue.

Kola nut
(Cola acuminata)

- **Parts used.** The seeds are used to make powder or tincture. The powder or seeds are used in infusion or tincture form diluted with water.
- This majestic tree is native to Africa where it has been used as a medicinal remedy and aphrodisiac.
- General stimulant that tones the nervous system and heart. It also helps to recover energy.
- Used for cases of psychological and physical fatigue and for nervous depression.
- **Warning.** Although this is a stimulant for the nervous system, in high doses it can have a depressing effect; it can produce over-excitement followed by depression.

Recommended doses:

- Infusion of powder made from seeds.
    Up to ¹/₂ teaspoon per cup.
    - Seed infusion. Use one teaspoon per cup of tea. Drink 2 cups a day before meals.
    - In tincture form. Drink up to 30 drops diluted in a glass of water, 3-4 times a day.

ENERGETIC WINE
Macerate 2 tablespoons of kola nut in 1 cup of high grade alcohol (in general 30 grades). After mixing add 3 cups of wine spirits and allow to age for 3 months. Filter and drink 3 small cups a day as a general tonic.

Rosemary
(Rosmarinus officinalis)

- **Parts used.** The leaves, fresh or dried are used in infusions. They are also used to make essential oils and medicinal tinctures.
- Native to the Mediterranean, it was used in ancient culture to improve and strengthen the memory.

• Used for cases of tiredness, stress and slight depression.

• Its aroma and flavor is penetrating and is used in cooking. It is said that rosemary "lifts up the spirit."

• Stimulates blood pressure, especially in the head, improving concentration. It also helps to relieve headaches, improves memory and restores and invigorates the body after a long tiring day.

FOR EXHAUSTION

• **Infusion for headache.** Take every 3 hours, 2 tablespoons of rosemary infusion prepared with dried leaves.

• **Revitalizing tincture.** Drink 1 teaspoon of tincture diluted in water, 2 times per day. It is an excellent tonic for the body.

ESSENTIAL OILS FROM A TO Z

LIMONCELLO OR LEMON HERB

Strengthens the body, and acts as an excellent muscular stimulant. This herb also helps to relieve the nervous exhaustion produced by tiredness. It also is good for headaches and exhaustion brought on by change of routines. Its aroma acts as a natural antidepressant. It can be blended with ginger and jasmine for a potent remedy.
Safety. If you use in baths and massages, it's important to use small doses because it can be irritating.

NIAULI

Physical and mental stimulant. Its tonic effects improve concentration and clear thinking. It's one of the most beneficial essential oils and it doesn't present side effects. It doesn't irritate the skin, always use high quality oil.
Safety. Because of its stimulant characteristics, it's best to use it in the afternoon, combined with other sedative oils, such as lavender and fennel so that it doesn't cause insomnia.

Sage
(Salvia officinalis)

- **Parts used.** The leaves, fresh or dried are used to make infusions, essential oils and medicinal tinctures.
- It is known as a plant used in cooking. In Mediterranean cuisine, the plant's native region, sage is a common herb. Its name is a key to its curative properties: it comes from the Latin word *salvare*, which means "to save."
- Its components act as a gentle stimulating tonic for the central nervous system, for which reason it gives relief for everyday tiredness.
- In Chinese medicine it is considered to be a yin tonic, which calms and at the same time stimulates the nervous system.
- **Warning.** Do not drink this remedy during pregnancy and breastfeeding, because it is a strong hormonal stimulant and one of its components, tuyona, disrupts the production of breast milk.

FOR EVERYDAY EXHAUSTION
Prepare an infusion with 1 tablespoon of sage flowers and leaves, add hot water to 1 cup, let sit for 5 minutes and strain. Drink 3 cups a day.

Yerba maté
(Ilex paraguaiensis)

- **Parts used.** The leaves, which contain active components. It is cultivated by cutting the branches, which doesn't harm the tree.
- This plant species is native to the bordering regions of Argentina, Brazil and Paraguay. The indigenous people of this region, the Guarani, chewed on maté leaves during the day and would drink this herb as a comforting elixir that gives strength and energy.
- *Yerba maté* is a stimulant to fight mental and physical fatigue. It supports intellectual work.

Yerba maté contains vitamin C, complex B vitamins and minerals such as calcium, potassium and magnesium.
• It doesn't present any side effects except in cases of nervousness and insomnia.

HOW TO DRINK YERBA MATÉ

This beverage can be used in two infusion forms:

• As a tea, by boiling water with 2 teaspoons of *yerba maté* (per cup) and draining before drinking.

• The most traditional way to drink *yerba maté* is in a small cup or gourd called *maté* through a *bombilla* (metal filter straw).

ESSENTIAL OILS FROM A TO Z

PINE

Its balsamic properties restore and invigorate the mind. It is used for cases of low self-esteem and other psychological symptoms caused by fatigue.

Safety. This oil can cause allergic reactions for some people and bronchial spasms in children. When used in excess this oil can cause hypertension.

ROMAN CAMOMILE

Powerful sedative for muscular pains caused by extreme tiredness. Its curative effects are not only physical but also psychological, because they are used for emotional problems caused by fatigue and stress. Can be combined with angelica and jasmine to make it more potent and to enrich a soft aromatic blend.

Safety. It shouldn't be used during the first four months of pregnancy.

Foods to fight fatigue

Tiredness is one of the symptoms which indicates an imbalance of energy which is the product of various factors. Excessive activity, lack of rest, poor physical condition and daily pressures can cause tiredness, but an unbalanced diet can be a key element in not being able to recuperate.

✚ Our bodies act as motors and if we lack fuel (a lack of necessary nutrients) we feel tired and can end up getting fatigued or ill.

Planning a balanced, nutrient diet rich in carbohydrates, proteins, minerals and vitamins is vital in fighting against extreme exhaustion. Iron rich foods like meat should be staples in your diet. You should also include a sufficient amount of vitamin C, found in fruits and vegetables, which can help to absorb iron and magnesium. A deficiency of magnesium can cause muscular weakness. At the same time it's advised to cut down on caffeine, which is a stimulating substance. Also, it is fundamental to drink enough liquids, at least 6 to 8 glasses of water per day. Calculate 3 to 5 glasses more for each hour of intense physical exercise, because dehydration can cause extreme fatigue.

WHAT YOU CAN'T LACK

Because of their vital functions in providing energy, iron and zinc are the minerals for a diet to fight tiredness.

Zinc

Essential for any age to maintain health, because it helps to support the break down of proteins, carbohydrates, fats and nucleic acids. It also helps to recharge energy after surgery and in cases of fever, states that tend to bring on cases of severe tiredness and chronic fatigue syndrome. A low level of zinc can aggravate illnesses, cause sleeping disorders, stunted growth, depression and loss of appetite. Found in **honey, fresh oysters, ginger, dried fruits, red meats** and **corn kernels**.

Iron

Essential mineral for the formation of hemoglobin, that transports oxygen around the body, strengthens the immune system and prevents certain types of anaemia that can cause tiredness. In addition, this mineral intervenes in the production of energy enzymes. It increases the bones' resistance and helps to develop the intellectual capacity. Present in **honey, liver, brewers' yeast, grains, dried fruits, sardines, spinach, eggs** and **cauliflower**.

NOTE
You should always consult your doctor before changing your diet.

HONEY

Honey is a natural sugar, which is different from refined sugar, it provides calories rich in minerals, especially iron and zinc. It also contains vitamins in the complex B group, vitamin C, sodium, calcium, phosphorus, and magnesium. It helps to balance the body, acts as an energizing tonic and at the same time relaxes the nervous and circulatory system. Used for moments of mental and physical exhaustion. The key to honey is in its simple (mono sucrose) sugars, a powerful source of energy that the blood absorbs in its original form.

DOSE AGAINST TIREDNESS

For cases of occasional fatigue and when recuperating from a prolonged illness it is recommended to take at least 4 teaspoons of honey a day, until you feel better. For slight cases of tiredness, take 1 teaspoon in the morning and another at night.

VITAMINS AND MINERALS

The vitamin B group

This vitamin group helps the functioning of the nervous system and the maintenance of mental health and metabolic energy. These vitamins are irreplaceable when recovering from exhaustion or fatigue.

■ B_1 Water-soluble nutrient that the body does not produce and needs to be incorporated into the diet. Helps to metabolize carbohydrates and improves digestion. Essential for energy, relieving states of tiredness and improving memory. Found in **sunflower seeds**, **beans**, **wholewheat breads**, **artichokes**, **celery**, **garlic** and other **vegetables**.

■ B_2 Helps to break down carbohydrates, proteins and fats, converting them into energy, this energy can be lost during periods of excessive tiredness. It also helps to protect the body against anaemia, migraines and cramping. It is found in **liver**, **almonds**, **dairy products** and **broccoli**.

■ B_3 The aminoacid tryptophan can be converted inside the human body to vitamin B_3, and is fundamental to produce energy. It contains enzymes that breakdown carbohydrates. It also regulates sugar in the blood, activates circulation, stimulates the nervous system and acts as an antioxidant.

SESAME AGAINST FATIGUE

The body needs iron to produce the pigment that transports oxygen. Iron is found in the body's red blood cells and is fundamental for the formation of hemoglobin, a protein that transports oxygen. It supports the breathing of the body's cells. Vegetarians who don't consume animal products, rich in iron, can substitute sesame seeds, a source rich in iron and also containing calcium, zinc, foliate and complex B vitamins and vitamin E. You can toast sesame seeds in a pan and add them to meat and fish. This recipe is great for sprinkling over soups, stews and salads.

As with other B-complex vitamins it can be found in **wholegrain cereals**, **fish**, **eggs**, **dates**, **peanuts**, **milk** and **coffee**.

■ **B$_4$** Acts in the functioning of supra-renal gland, which is activated when you are exhausted or under stress. It helps the body break down carbohydrates and proteins. It is helpful in cases of stress and exhaustion. Good sources of B$_5$ are **dairy products**, **eggs**, **peanuts**, **walnuts**, **avocado** and **lentils**.

■ **B$_6$** It is an important vitamin for the immune system. It supports the metabolism, helps to balance hormones and breaks down fats and carbohydrates. It helps to prevent extreme tiredness and muscular cramps. It is found in **sunflower seeds**, **dried fruits**, **bananas**, **chicken** and **coffee**.

■ **B$_{12}$** It's important for avoiding cases of fatigue and for maintaining the health of the nervous system, improving concentration and memory. It helps to prevent anaemia and to

MEAT: IRON + VITAMIN B

Red meat is essential for iron and vitamin B$_{12}$, which is essential for the formation and maintenance of the nervous system, and helps increase your resistance to fatigue. Other meats, including fish and poultry, and eggs give similar benefits. They are rich in proteins, stimulate the brain and improve the mind's function.

keep the body's health balanced. Found in **meat-derived** foods and some vegetables: **liver, oysters, salmon, eggs, cheese, fortified cereals** and **brewers' yeast**.

Vitamin C

Prevents anaemia (because it helps to absorb iron), gastroduodenal ulcers and immune deficiencies. It is an anti-oxidant increasing the production of collagen, which helps to prevent premature aging. An anti-histamine, it is used for cases of allergies. **Warning.** Excess vitamin C supplements can provoke diarrhea. Found in **fruits** and **vegetables** like **apricots, lemon, broccoli, green** and **red peppers, potatoes, currants** and **guavas**.

Calcium

Promotes well-being, and excites the nerves and muscles. It also helps to relieve anxiety, regulate sleep and heart rhythm. Found in: **milk, cheese, yogurt, cider vinegar, sardines, leafy greens** and **sesame seeds**.

LEMON

A citrus fruit, which is not eaten whole, but used in cooking and for medicinal and aesthetic remedies. Contains energizing components that activate the body's flow of fluids, which is good for cases of tiredness. Contains vitamin C, B_1 and B_2 and minerals such as potassium, calcium, magnesium and phosphorus.

REMEDY FOR TIREDNESS

Juice I lemon, take out the seeds and add sugar and water. Drink to fight extreme fatigue, to give you an instant pick-me-up.
Safety. Those who suffer from gastritis or gastric acid should use lemon in moderation.

CIDER VINEGAR

This is a fermented product derived from apples, which has rejuvenating and curative properties. Helps to keep a healthy level of acids in the body, which tend to plummet when exhausted. Contains calcium, magnesium, sodium, phosphorus, cilium and potassium.

REFRESHING VINEGAR

Mix 1 glass of water, 2 spoonfuls of cider vinegar and 1 spoon of honey. Mix together and drink small sips. This beverage is recommended for cases of extreme exhaustion and as a daily energizer for athletes.

APRICOTS

Fresh or dried apricots are rich in vitamin C, potassium, fiber, iron and calcium. Dried apricots contain five times more potassium than fresh apricots. It's recommended to eat dried fruits in cases of exhaustion or when exercising. Apricot sauce is recommended when you feel tired, because it contains a high amount of potassium.

ENERGETIC DOSE FOR WOMEN

6 dried apricots provide about 13 percent of the recommended daily amount of iron for women. Eating apricots daily helps to energize your body and prevent anaemia.

Phosphorus

Found in the body's cells, it is the most abundant mineral in the body after calcium. It is necessary for the chemical reaction in the body to capture, transfer and store energy, for the formation of the bone structure and for the nervous system and brain functions. A lack of phosphorus can cause weakness, mental confusion, loss of appetite, anaemia and general low resistance to

PHOSPHORUS RICH DIET

Any of the following combinations of foods provides the recommended daily dose of phosphorus:

- *Ample portion of fish, 2 glasses of skim milk;*
- *1 cup of firm tofu, 1 portion of cheese, 1 ham sandwich;*
- *1 portion of lean red meat, 1 egg, 1 portion of cheese;*
- *1 cup of cooked lentils, 1 spoonful of cottage cheese, 1 spoonful of brewers' yeast, 1 egg.*

ENERGETIC SMOOTHY FOR CHILDREN

Blend in a blender 4 pears and 2 bananas with powdered milk and sugar. Blend for 2 minutes and serve with crushed ice. This refreshing drink is a yummy treat for kids and all ages.

illnesses. Absorption of phosphorus is increased with calcium and vitamin D. Found in **honey, white fish, brewers' yeast, dairy products, cereals, walnuts, figs, mushrooms, onion** and **cauliflower**.

Magnesium

Vital for the cellular function that helps the body to produce energy. Supports the muscular and cardiac functions and transmits nervous impulses. It is recommended for cases of exhaustion. Found in **meats, walnuts, milk, maize, sesame seeds, chestnuts, broccoli, almonds** and **grapes**.

Potassium

Provides an essential nutrients for cellular function helping to produce energy in the body, because it helps to stabilize heart rhythm and blood pressure, remove toxins and regulates activity in the intestines and kidneys. It also influences muscle and nervous activity, helping to keep a healthy balance of fluids. Can easily be lost when sweating during physical activities, it is also used as a diuretic. A lack of potassium can cause excessive fatigue, heart palpitations, confusion and depression. Found in **bananas, pears, grapes, apple cider vinegar, salmon** and some **vegetables**.

PEARS

Carbohydrates found in pears are slowly released in the body, which helps to keep up the body's energy level. It's an ideal food for athletes or if you exercise a lot. Contains high levels of potassium, soluble fiber and beta-carotene.
It has been proven that the oligo element called boro improves brain activity.

GRAPES

Grapes are considered one of the best fruits because their components stimulate neurons, increase vital energy and tone the blood. The main nutrient found in grapes is potassium, but they also contain proteins, sodium, magnesium, iron and phosphorus. With therapeutic effects, it is used as a decoction, juice or ground.

Safety. Contain high amounts of sugar. When eaten in excessive amounts can cause feelings of anguish, disillusion and sympthoms of diarrhea. Not recommended for cases of diabetes.

TONIC FOR VITAL ENERGY

Extract grape juice and place over fire until it forms a syrup. Mix with an equal amount of honey, let cool and place in a bottle. Drink 1 tablespoon, mixed with water twice a day.

index

LIVE
LIKE A KING

This book belongs
to the
Mabel Brigham - Murray
Circle
of the
First Presbyterian Church
of
Edmond, Oklahoma

Given to
Sharon Finley
From the above Circle.

1984

LIVE
LIKE A KING

By

WARREN W. WIERSBE

---

*Making the Beatitudes work in
daily life*

MOODY PRESS

CHICAGO

Library of Congress Cataloging in Publication Data

Wiersbe, Warren W.
  Live like a king!

  1. Beatitudes. I. Title.

BT382.W53   226'.93'06   76-17576
ISBN: 0-8024-4907-7

9 10 11 12 Printing/ML/Year 87 86 85 84 83

My wife and I have enjoyed the fellowship of many friends in the ministry, and with affection and appreciation, I dedicate this book to some of them:

> Jim and Betty Gurley
> Joe and Dorothy Guthrie
> Gaylard and Ruth Hamilton
> Bruce and Verla Love
> Ken and Thelma McQuere
> Pete and Alice Quist

"Even as it is meet for me to think this of you all, because I have you in my heart."

PHILIPPIANS 1:7

Contents

Preface

THESE CHAPTERS are based on a series of messages I delivered at The Moody Church during the summer of 1975. Many who heard them expressed a desire to have them in permanent form. However, let me hasten to point out that in these chapters I have taken a somewhat different approach from the original sermons. I wish now I could preach the series again!

I recognize the fact that the Sermon on the Mount has both present and future implications. It is the former that are emphasized here. In the entire series of studies, I have tried to help the believer today realize what it means to "reign in life" through Jesus Christ. I believe that God wants each of His children to live like a king, and that the Beatitudes help point the way to that experience.

Knowing the imperfections of both the author and the book, I tremble as I send these pages forth. But if they help some believer enter more fully into the privileges of the throne, then I will consider the work rewarded. "Brethren, I count not myself to have apprehended" (Philippians 3:13).

1

Are You Walking or Riding?

IMAGINE what it would be like to present King Solomon on a TV talk show. He was "wiser than all men" (1 Kings 4:31) and was the composer of over a thousand songs and the author of three thousand proverbs. (Think of the books and records he could sell!) He could intelligently discuss trees, animals, birds, insects, and fish; and he was no ignoramus when it came to buildings, horses, money, or (sad to say) women. He was a keen observer of the world around him and was able to draw wisdom from events that would appear very insignificant to other people.

Like the day he looked out his window and saw some travelers go by, some walking and some riding horses. He wrote in his journal: "There is an evil which I have seen under the sun, as an error which proceedeth from the ruler: folly is set in great dignity, and the rich sit in low place. I have seen servants upon horses, and princes walking as servants upon the earth" (Ecclesiastes 10:5-7).

Princes are supposed to ride on horses, and their servants are supposed to walk beside them. But Solomon saw the situation reversed: those who were supposed to serve were ruling, and those who were supposed to rule were serving! The world was topsy-turvy—and it still is today.

Take, for example, the marvellous machine we call the human body. God made it to be the servant of the spirit, but in the lives of many people it is the master. The appetites ride on horseback while the spirit trudges along on foot. The same reverse situation exists when it comes to money and material things. God gave them to us to be our servants, but somehow they have become our masters.

In other words, too many people are walking when they should be riding.

God created us to be kings, and everything else to be our servants. The fact that we are created in the image of God is proof enough of this statement. But God's words to the first man and woman make our kingship even more exciting: "Be fruitful, and multiply, and replenish the earth, and subdue it: and have dominion over the fish of the sea, and over the fowl of the air, and over every living thing that moveth upon the earth" (Genesis 1:28). *"Have dominion."* This simply means, "Live like a king!" Our first parents were not simply tenants in Paradise; they were the rulers!

"If God created us to be kings," you are no doubt asking at this point, "then—what happened? Man certainly doesn't have dominion over the fish and fowl and animals today. For that matter, he doesn't even have dominion over *himself!"*

A good question. What did happen so that man stopped living like a king and started living like a servant? When did he get off the horse and start walking? *When he disobeyed God.* When Adam and Eve deliberately disobeyed God's commandment, they went from sovereigns to sinners to servants. They lost their crowns. They got off the horse and started walking and became the servants instead of the rulers. And, sad to say, every child of Adam (and that means all of us) is born a slave.

Can we do anything to change the situation? Yes, we can. For, just as God the Father created us to be kings, God the Son redeemed us to be kings. In His death, burial, and resurrection, Jesus Christ undid all that Adam's sin accomplished—and much more! The dominion that was lost through Adam's disobedience has been regained through Christ's obedience, and there is no longer any need for you and me to be walking like servants. Romans 5:17 puts it so beautifully: "For if by one man's [Adam's] offense death reigned by one; much more they which receive abundance of grace and of the gift of righteousness shall reign in life by one, Jesus Christ."

Note those key words: "they . . . shall reign in life." Who shall reign in life? Those who have received God's free gift of grace and righteousness in Jesus Christ. And it does not say "reign in death" or "reign in the future Kingdom." It says *reign in life!* That means living like a king right here and now!

In my ministry I have met many slaves who have become kings by yielding themselves to Jesus Christ. I remember Harry, who, with his wife, stopped at the church study one Friday afternoon. He was a church member, but he was also an alcoholic. Nobody knew it except Harry and his wife and a few close drinking pals. This had been going on for years. Harry would work hard at his job all week and never touch a drop. Then Friday night would arrive, and he would take off for the tavern. He would be "under the influence" all that night and all day Saturday and would sober up in time to be in Sunday school Sunday morning.

"I'm sick of it," he told me. "Tell me what to do."

I told him what to do: "Harry, you've got to turn yourself over to Jesus Christ and let Him be the Lord of your life."

He did it—and the change was immediate! He got back on the horse and started living like a king. And not only that, but he devoted himself to helping other men find their true kingship in Jesus Christ. Whenever I was called upon by anybody having problems with alcohol, I always sent him to Harry, because he could help him better than I could. The last I heard, Harry was still riding on the horse, and his body was his servant instead of his master.

God the Father created you to be a king, and God the Son redeemed you to be a king; and God the Spirit can empower you to be a king. We "reign in life" through the power of the Spirit of God. "For it is God which worketh in you both to will and to do of his good pleasure" (Philippians 2:13). "Now unto him that is able to do exceeding abundantly above all that we ask or think, according to the power that worketh in us" (Ephesians 3:20). If left to ourselves, we fail; but if we yield to the indwelling Holy Spirit, we succeed. He alone can empower us to live like kings.

So, the question you must answer is, Am I walking or riding? Or, to put it another way, Am I serving my servants, or are they serving me? Are you ruling over the appetites of the body? Are you in control of money and material things? (Money is a wonderful servant but a terrible master.) Are you reigning in life?

You can.

This is what the Beatitudes are all about. They explain how you can reign in life and live like a king. Most people think of the Beatitudes as a collection of idealistic sayings, beautiful to read but impossible to practice. How wrong they are! In fact, the entire Sermon on the Mount is a glorious explanation of what life is really like when you reign through the power of the Holy Spirit. Dr. G. Campbell Morgan called the Sermon on the Mount "The Manifesto of the King," and that is just what it is. Jesus Christ the King is telling us how to live like kings! He is explaining how to reign over such servants as *ego,* so that you practice humility and not pride; *power,* so that you build up and do not destroy; *appetite,* so that you crave purity and not sin. The Beatitudes tell you how to get back in the saddle so that you are riding like a king and not trudging like a slave.

Believe me: you can live like a king—provided you know Jesus Christ as your Saviour and will completely yield to Him. We "reign in life by one, Jesus Christ" (Romans 5:17). Jesus Christ is the only King that God will recognize. Jesus was born a King; "Where is he that is born King of the Jews?" (Matthew 2:2). He lived as a King in spite of the opposition of wicked men and Satan himself.

Since Adam, Jesus Christ is the only Man to walk this earth and exercise the kind of dominion that God originally gave us when He created us. For example, Jesus had dominion over the fish of the sea. He gave Peter a great catch of fish when it seemed impossible to catch anything (Luke 5:1-11); and He even brought one fish to Peter's hook when the apostle had to pay his Temple tax (Matthew 17:24-27). Jesus also had dominion over the fowl of the air. He kept every bird in Jerusalem quiet until the cock was supposed to crow announcing Peter's denial of Christ. Jesus even had dominion over the beasts of the field. During His temptation, He was in the wilderness "with the wild beasts" (Mark 1:13); and He rode into Jerusalem on a colt "whereon never man sat" (Mark 11:2). Jesus Christ is the Last Adam, exercising the dominion lost by the disobedience of the first Adam—and He wants to share that dominion with you and me!

Jesus Christ was born a King, He lived as a King, and He died as a King. True, the only crown He wore was a mocking crown of thorns; and His only throne was a cross bearing the inscription, "This is the King of the Jews." To human eyes, His crucifixion seemed like defeat; but to the King, it meant victory. His supreme act of sovereignty was laying down His life for the sins of the world. He was not murdered; He willingly gave His life as your Substitute and mine. Never was His Kingship more evident than in Gethsemane and at Golgotha, where He was "obedient unto death, even the death of the cross" (Philippians 2:8). The greatest test of our kingship is how we use our authority. Jesus used His authority to save others, even though it meant He could not save Himself.

Today Jesus Christ reigns as King, for God "raised him from the dead, and set him at his own right hand in the heavenly places, far above all" (Ephesians 1:20-21). "For he must reign, till he hath put all enemies under his feet" (1 Corinthians 15:25).

The tragedy is, too many people echo that rebellious cry of centuries ago, "We will not have this man to reign over us" (Luke 19:14). This rebellion is the explanation for the problems in our world today: men think they are free when, in reality, they are slaves. "The kings of the earth set themselves, and the rulers take counsel together, against the LORD, and against his anointed, saying, Let us break their bands asunder, and cast away their cords from us" (Psalm 2:2-3). But in rejecting Christ and refusing to submit to God's Word, men are only forfeiting their own kingship. We reign in life by submitting to the authority of God. George Matheson expresses it perfectly:

> My will is not my own
> Til Thou hast made it Thine;
> If it would reach the monarch's throne
> It must its crown resign.

God the Father created you to be a king, and you cannot enjoy the fulfillment of your life until you experience this kingship through Jesus Christ. God the Son redeemed you to be a king, but you cannot reign in life until He is your Saviour and Lord. God the Spirit can enable you to live like a king, but His power is limited until you yield your all to Him. Your kingship depends on your relationship to God, and your relationship to God depends on the decision of your own will.

"I have seen servants upon horses, and princes walking as servants upon the earth."

You were meant to be a king.

Are you walking or riding?

2

The King Is Here!

I

THE BEATITUDES are part of what we call the Sermon on the Mount, and the Sermon on the Mount is a part of the gospel of Matthew, which is the "Gospel of the King." If we are going to understand the message of the Beatitudes, then we are going to have to know something about both the gospel of Matthew and the Sermon on the Mount. Matthew 1:1 is a key verse: "The book of the generation of Jesus Christ, the son of David, the son of Abraham."

The Old Testament is "the book of the generations of Adam" (Genesis 5:1), and, of course, Adam was the first king in human history. God blessed Adam and gave him "dominion over the fish of the sea, and over the fowl of the air, and over every living thing that moveth upon the earth" (Genesis 1:28). But no man has a right to rule over others who cannot rule over himself. This explains why God tested Adam; for if Adam was to be God's king, he had to be *under* authority before he could *exercise* authority.

Adam failed, and his sin plunged the human race into depravity and death. When you read "the book of the generations of Adam," you find failure in generation after generation. Abraham lied about his wife, and so did his son, Isaac. Jacob was a schemer, and Moses was a murderer. David was an adulterer and a murderer. And these men were the spiritual leaders of the Jewish nation! No wonder the Old Testament ends with the ominous words, "lest I come and smite the earth with a curse" (Malachi 4:6).

What a relief it is to turn to the gospel of Matthew and enter a new book, "The book of the generation of Jesus Christ, the son of David, the son of Abraham" (Matthew 1:1). Here is God's new King! And unlike the first Adam, Jesus Christ, the "last Adam" (1 Corinthians 15:45), obeyed God and therefore was able to exercise dominion. Because He was under authority, He was able to exercise authority . The first Adam was tested in a beautiful garden, and he failed; but the Last Adam was tested in a dangerous wilderness, and He succeeded. Because the first Adam was a thief, he was cast out of Paradise; but the Last Adam turned to a thief on a cross and said, "To day shalt thou be with me in paradise" (Luke 23:43). "The book of the generations of Adam" ends with a curse; but the "book of the generation of Jesus Christ" ends with the promise, "And there shall be no more curse" (Revelation 22:3).

You and I were born the first time into "the generations of Adam," and this made us sinners and slaves. When you are born again through faith in Jesus Christ, you enter "the generation of Jesus Christ," and you are born a child of God *and a king!* "Unto him that loved us, and washed us from our sins in his own blood, and hath made us kings and priests unto God and his Father" (Revelation 1:5-6). Because we belong to the family of the King, we can "reign in life by one, Jesus Christ" (Romans 5:17).

The gospel of Matthew presents Jesus Christ as God's King. In the first ten chapters, Matthew answers the three questions anyone would ask about a king: Where did he come from? What does he believe? What can he do? In Matthew 1-4, the Person of the King is presented—His background, birth, baptism, and temptation. In these chapters we are assured that Jesus Christ is the Son of God, sent by the Father to be the Saviour of the world. In Matthew 5-7, the Sermon on the Mount, we have the Principles of the King, what He believes and what He wants to do in our lives. Chapters 8-10 reveal the Power of the King and show us our Lord's power over demons, disease, and even death. In other words, in Jesus Christ we have the perfect King! When you trust Him as your Saviour, He sets you free from sin and judgment, and He enables you to reign in life and enjoy His spiritual Kingdom here and now.

II

But what kind of a Kingdom do we share as we yield to Christ and reign in life? The answer to that question is given in what we call the Sermon on the Mount. It is unfortunate that this magnificent sermon has been robbed of its importance by people applying it only to the Jews or only to some future period in God's prophetic plan. It is my conviction that the Sermon on the Mount applies to Christians today, and only to Christians. To apply it to unsaved nations is to twist the Scriptures; and to move it into some future age is to rob it of its spiritual power today. I might add that the purpose of the Sermon on the Mount is not evangelism, although certainly the Spirit could use it to give light to a seeking sinner. (I have a Jewish friend who was converted reading the genealogy in Matthew 1, but I do not recommend you add that chapter to your bag of tools for soul winning!) The Sermon on the Mount was given to explain to the disciples the kind of Kingdom Jesus wants to build in the lives of His followers.

When our Lord began His ministry, there were several groups in Palestine that claimed to have the answer to Israel's problems. The Pharisees claimed that the nation could experience freedom and blessing only if the people returned to the traditions of the fathers. The Sadducees, on the other hand, urged the people to update their religion and become more liberal. The Essenes taught that salvation would come only through separation from the world, so they established their little communities and remained outside the life of the nation. At the other extreme were the Zealots, a revolutionary group that sought to overthrow Rome by revolt and force. Unwilling to wait for gradual change, the Zealots murdered and destroyed in the name of Jewish patriotism.

If you look deeply enough, you will see that we have similar groups today. We have those who cry, "Go back!" and attempt to return us to "the good old days" of our fathers. Another group cries, "Go ahead!" and urges us to modernize and liberalize our religion and our philosophy of life. The radical extremists shout, "Go against!" and try to destroy vital institutions necessary for the strength and progress of society. The separatists say, "Go out!" and isolate themselves from the very people who may need their help. The names of the groups will change from generation to generation, but the basic aims are the same.

In contrast to all these solutions to the human problem is what Jesus calls the Kingdom of God, or the Kingdom of heaven. (Matthew seems to prefer "Kingdom of heaven" because his Jewish readers would fear to pronounce the name of God.) In the Sermon on the Mount, Jesus says, "All of these approaches are right in some respects and wrong in other respects. Their chief weakness is that they are fragmentary: they each deal with a facet of truth but not with the whole of truth."

For example, there is nothing wrong with the traditions of the fathers. But the Old Testament Law was temporary; it was preparation for the coming of the Messiah, Jesus Christ. We cannot duplicate today the religion of Israel under the Old Covenant. Instead, we must let this Old Testament truth develop into New Testament truth through Jesus Christ. This is why He said, "Think not that I am come to destroy the law, or the prophets: I am not come to destroy, but to fulfil" (Matthew 5:17). The Old Testament Law was the seed; the Gospel of Christ is the fruit. You can destroy a seed by pulverizing it with a hammer, or by planting it in the ground and letting it fulfill its purpose by becoming a plant. It destroys itself by fulfilling itself. This is how Jesus Christ fulfilled the Law: He brought it to its fruition in His life, death, and resurrection;

and now "the righteousness of the law [is] fulfilled in us, who walk not after the flesh, but after the Spirit" (Romans 8:4).

If the Pharisees wanted to hold on to the past and reject the present, the Sadducees went to the other extreme: they wanted to take the rational approach to life and sacrifice the authority of the Word on the altar of intellectual credibility. They were the modernists of their day. Jesus agreed with them that the Word must be a living reality today, but He rejected their anti-supernatural approach. "For the Sadducees say that there is no resurrection, neither angel, nor spirit" (Acts 23:8). When the Sadducees tried to trip Him up with their theological questions, Jesus swept them aside with one devastating statement: "Ye do err, not knowing the scriptures, nor the power of God" (Matthew 22:29). It is through the Word of God and the power of God by His Spirit that the believer today experiences the reign of God in his life. The Pharisees lost the present by trying to return to the past. The Sadducees lost the present by denying the past. Both were wrong.

Jesus would have sympathized with the Essenes in their desire for holy living, but He would have rejected their isolationism. If the Sermon on the Mount emphasizes anything, it is that sin is a matter of the heart and not just the outward actions. One does not have to murder to be a sinner; all he has to do is hate (Matthew 5:21-26). And you can carry a hateful heart into the desert wastes with you! Years ago, a religious college announced in its catalog: "Our campus is located forty miles from any known sin." What a preposterous claim! The Sermon on the Mount emphasizes holy living, but not at the expense of the normal duties and demands of human life. A change in geography is no guarantee of an improvement in character.

As for the Zealots, Jesus chose one of their number to be one of His disciples: "Simon called Zelotes" (Luke 6:15). Imagine selecting a political fanatic to be among the first disciples! No doubt Jesus admired their zeal and devotion, just as He certainly opposed their violent methods. He would say to Simon, "Yes, some things in 'the establishment' need to be destroyed, but not through hatred, violence, and human force. The weapons we use are not of the flesh; they are of the spirit. It is not by killing others but by being willing to die yourself that you will establish God's Kingdom."

So the Sermon on the Mount has for its theme our Lord's statement in Matthew 5:20, "For I say unto you, That except your righteousness shall exceed the righteousness of the scribes and Pharisees, ye shall in no case enter into the kingdom of heaven."

III

What was wrong with the righteousness of the scribes and Pharisees? For one thing, they thought that holiness was only a matter of outward actions, and they ignored the inward attitudes of the heart. Their righteousness was only external, a safe system of dos and don'ts by which they could measure their spirituality. In one of His parables, Jesus has the Pharisee pray: "I thank thee, that I am not as other men are, extortioners, unjust, adulterers, or even as this publican. I fast twice in the week, I give tithes of all that I possess" (Luke 18:11-12). Certainly there is nothing good about being an extortioner or an adulterer, and there is nothing bad about fasting or tithing. But if this is the whole of a man's religion, he has nothing! And if he is proud of it to the point of looking down upon a fellow sinner, then he is in bad condition spiritually!

In the Beatitudes, Jesus teaches us that true righteousness is a matter of the heart. It has been well said, "The Beatitudes describe the *attitudes* that ought to *be* in the believer's life." What good are tithing, fasting, and outward obedience to rules and regulations if the heart is proud, critical, and condemning? Conduct must be based upon character. "For man looketh on the outward appearance, but the LORD looketh on the heart" (1 Samuel 16:7). "Keep thy heart with all diligence; for out of it are the issues of life" (Proverbs 4:23).

In Matthew 5:21-48, Jesus illustrates this basic principle that righteousness must be a matter of the heart. He takes some of the traditions of the elders and shows how inadequate they are. "Thou shalt not kill" involves much more than physical violence: hatred in the heart is the equivalent of murder with the hand. "Thou shalt not commit adultery" involves much more than an immoral act: cultivating the desire in the heart is the equivalent of adultery. The Sermon on the Mount goes much deeper than the Ten Commandments; for, with one exception ("Thou shalt not covet"), the Ten Commandments deal only with outward actions, while the Sermon on the Mount deals with inward attitudes. In the Sermon on the Mount, Jesus not only breaks away the shell of Pharisaic tradition that covered God's Law, but He also penetrates to the heart of that Law and explains its deeper, spiritual meaning. The Word of God is like seed. The Pharisees put a "crust" of tradition around the seed so that it could not give life and bear fruit. Jesus breaks that crust and then opens the husk of the seed so the spiritual life can be fulfilled in us.

The Beatitudes, then, are a description of true righteousness in contrast to the false righteousness of the scribes and Pharisees. If we are going to live like kings, then we must manifest this kind of character; and we can do it only through the power of the Holy Spirit of God. Interestingly enough, the Holy Spirit is not even mentioned in these chapters; yet it is obvious that the believer could never in his own power attain this high level of Christian experience. "For what the law could not do, in that it was weak through the flesh, God sending his own Son in the likeness of sinful flesh, and for sin, condemned sin in the flesh: that the righteousness of the law might be fulfilled in us, who walk not after the flesh, but after the Spirit" (Romans 8: 3-4).

Not only were the Pharisees and scribes mistaken about righteousness and sin, but they were also mistaken in their motives for serving God; and Jesus deals with this error in Matthew 6. The Pharisees and scribes were religious in order to get the approval and praise of men. But the true Christian has a greater motive than that: he lives for the approval and praise of God. After all, if true righteousness is a matter of the heart, and only God can see the heart, then only God can give the reward. "I am he which searcheth the reins and hearts" (Revelation 2:23). Jesus warns us in Matthew 6 not to "do righteousness"—whether it be giving, fasting, or praying—in order to be seen of men. He says, "Live your life before the eye of God, not the eyes of men. Your Father sees in secret, and that is sufficient. If you live for the praise of men, you have your reward."

The Beatitudes, then, are God's description of Christian character, the kind of character that leads to the right conduct. When the Pharisee wondered because Jesus did not go through the ceremonial washing of hands at dinner, Jesus said to him: "Now you Pharisees have the habit of cleaning the outside of your cups and dishes, but inside you yourselves are full of greed and wickedness. You fools! Did not the One who made the outside make the inside too? But dedicate once for all your inner self, and at once you will have everything clean" (Luke 11:39-41, Williams). If there is dirty water coming out of the faucet, I do not buy a new faucet: I cleanse the cistern.

IV

In this book, we will consider the Beatitudes individually; but there is a truth to be gained by first considering them collectively. To begin with, the Beatitudes show us how to enter the Kingdom. The first step is admitting my spiritual bankruptcy and having a humble, honest attitude toward myself. "Blessed are the poor in spirit" applies the ax to the very root of pharisaical pride and hypocrisy. "Blessed are they that mourn" deals with my attitude toward my sin: instead of criticizing the other man, I judge myself. "Blessed are the meek" deals with my attitude toward God: I am submissive to Him and not trying to impress Him with who I am or what I have done. When I "hunger and thirst after righteousness," then God provides that righteousness in the person of His Son, Jesus Christ. Like the Pharisee Saul of Tarsus, I exchange my own self-righteousness for the grace-righteousness of Christ (Philippians 3:1-11).

But this is more than a commercial transaction, for the results can be seen in everyday life. Having received the righteousness of Christ, I can begin to manifest in my life the very character of God. I become merciful instead of condemning; I seek to cultivate purity of heart; I become a peacemaker, not a troublemaker. As I grow to become more like Christ, I experience the kind of treatment He received when He was on earth—reviling, persecution, false accusations. But because of His grace, I become salt and light in a world that is decayed and dark. Having entered the Kingdom, it is now my privilege to enlarge the Kingdom by applying His righteousness in the world about me.

This means that the Beatitudes are practically meaningless to the person who has never trusted Jesus Christ as Saviour. They may illustrate an ideal, but that ideal can never be reached in human strength alone. But the person who begins with "Blessed are the poor in spirit" should ultimately come to that place of trusting the Saviour. "To this man will I look," says the Lord, "even to him that is poor and of a contrite spirit, and trembleth at my word" (Isaiah 66:2).

The Beatitudes tell us how to enter the Kingdom and enlarge the Kingdom; but they also tell us how to enjoy the Kingdom. "Blessed are . . . for they shall—" They shall what? Just read the promises, and you will see how much the believer enjoys from God when he seeks to cultivate true Christian character. "Theirs is the kingdom"—authority. "They shall be comforted"—encouragement. "They shall inherit the earth"—provision for every need. "They shall be filled"—satisfaction. "They shall obtain mercy"—provision for ministry to others. "They shall see God"—spiritual vision. "They shall be called the children of God"—becoming more like God in daily life. There is a price to pay, but the results are well worth it.

Jesus Christ invites you and me into a life of enrichment and enlargement.

Will we pay the price?

Blessed are the poor in spirit: for their's is the kingdom of heaven.

Matthew 5:3

Except ye be converted, and become as little children, ye shall not enter into the kingdom of heaven.

Matthew 18:3

Every one that exalteth himself shall be abased; and he that humbleth himself shall be exalted.

Luke 18:14

Humble yourselves therefore under the mighty hand of God, that he may exalt you in due time.

1 Peter 5:6

God resisteth the proud, but giveth grace unto the humble.

James 4:6

3

The Poor in Spirit

I

WHAT DOES IT MEAN to be "poor in spirit"?

Most assuredly, it does not mean being poor-spirited. Unfortunately, there are some people who have little or no self-esteem and whose self-image is very poor; as a consequence their inner man is anemic.

I once counseled a young man who during childhood had heard nothing from his father but, "You are good for nothing and will never amount to anything!" The young man had such a low opinion of himself that he failed in everything he attempted, and every failure only added to his emotional and spiritual bankruptcy. I pointed out to him that he was important to God and therefore ought to have more self-esteem. After all, he was created in the image of God. Even more, Jesus Christ died for Him and the Holy Spirit lived in him—so he was worth something! All of this theology he accepted with his mind, but down in his heart he could still hear his father telling him how worthless he was.

Some people are shy and retiring by nature, but this is not the same as being poor in spirit. God created us with different temperaments and personalities; and some of us are extroverts, while others are introverts. But it is possible to be an introvert and be proud and an extrovert and be humble. Peter was certainly an extrovert, and Thomas was probably an introvert; yet Thomas's refusal to accept the fact of Christ's resurrection—

and his demand for proof!—was just as much an evidence of pride as Peter's boasting and poor swordsmanship. Shyness is not poverty of spirit.

Nor is that detestable, groveling attitude that we call mock humility. The classic example is Uriah Heep, in *David Copperfield,* who was always reminding people that he was "but a very 'umble person." In a more refined way, we see this mock humility in the person who denies about himself what everybody else knows is true. I once worked with a Sunday school teacher who had a great gift of working with children, yet she would deny it every time it was mentioned. "Oh, I can't do anything!" she would protest. "I just struggle along until somebody comes to do the job the way it ought to be done!" All of us in the meetings would just smile at each other and change the subject. We knew that her "protesting too much" was a veiled request for praise, and none of us felt like praising her. In a sense, Moses was guilty of this sin when he told God he was not able to speak. Who can tell God anything about himself that God does not already know? And, after all, God made us, and God is able to empower us to do whatever He calls us to do. Denying that we can accomplish God's work is not humility; it is the worst kind of pride!

To be poor in spirit means knowing yourself, accepting yourself, and being yourself to the glory of God.

It means *knowing* yourself—your strengths and weaknesses, your hidden desires, your ambitions, your spiritual gifts and natural abilities—and being honest about yourself. When I was in grade school, I almost developed an emotional disorder over sports. Both of my older brothers are capable athletes, but I am not; and every single time the boys in my class chose up sides, I was the last one chosen. At first it was a painful experience, for, after all, every schoolboy dreams of being a great baseball or football star. Then it got to be a joke, and finally I was able to accept the fact that I would never be a great athlete, or even a good player. One of my coaches was sure he could make a trackman out of me, but after I knocked over six hurdles and fractured my ankle, he changed his mind. Sometimes getting to know yourself can be a painful experience, but it is a part of maturing.

It also means *accepting* yourself. Some people, when they discover what they really are, deny their discovery and move into a life of pretending. In fact, some people have pretended their way right into a dream world of psychological problems and have completely lost touch with reality. Most of us do not go that far, but the inability to accept yourself can have serious emotional and spiritual consequences. When you accept yourself, you find it easier to accept others and also easier to accept God's plan for your life. It did not take me long to accept the fact that I was neither an athlete nor a mechanic. (I handle a hammer about as well as I do a baseball bat.) But early in my grade-school career I discovered a flair for words, and I have been speaking them and writing them ever since.

Being poor in spirit means knowing yourself, accepting yourself, and *being* yourself to the glory of God. Your best self, of course, and not something less. This means constant growing in every area of your life. It means using your strengths to overcome your weaknesses and using your weaknesses to discover in a new way the mighty power of God. "When I am weak, then am I strong" (2 Corinthians 12:10). Being yourself involves yielding to the Spirit of God and permitting Him to fulfill God's will in your life. You are not imitating somebody else or envying somebody else. You are yourself—your best self—empowered by the Spirit of God to do what God has called you to do.

To be poor in spirit means knowing that in myself, I am bankrupt, but in Christ, I am rich. It means discovering the place God wants me to fill and filling it for His glory, no matter how insignificant or unimportant I may think it is. The person who is truly poor in spirit knows that *every* place of God's choosing is an important place. "And the eye cannot say unto the hand, I have no need of thee: nor again the head to the feet, I have no need of you" (1 Corinthians 12:21). The believer who is poor in spirit is in the place of God's choosing, fulfilling the purpose of God's choosing and depending on the power that God alone can supply.

Perhaps the word *humility* is another way of saying "poor in spirit." I think it was Andrew Murray who said that humility is that grace that, when you know you have it, you have lost it! He also said, "Humility is not thinking meanly of yourself. It is simply not thinking of yourself at all!" This explains why "Blessed are the poor in spirit" is the first of the Beatitudes; for until we admit our need, we can never receive what God has for us. Too many people are like those in the Laodicean church; they are "rich, and increased with goods, and have need of nothing" (Revelation 3:17). And, like the Laodiceans, they know not that they are "wretched, and miserable, and poor, and blind, and naked."

To be poor in spirit does not mean to deny your personality or try to suppress it. It simply means yielding it to God for Him to make it all that He wants it to be. The motto is old but true: "God always gives His best to those who leave the choice with Him."

II

There are several evidences of humility in the life of the believer. To begin with, when you are poor in spirit, you *accept others, because you have accepted yourself.* This does not mean you always agree with what they are or what they do, but you accept them just the same. When others succeed, you are happy for them; when they fail, you try to encourage them. If I find myself happy when they fail and sad when they succeed, then I am not poor in spirit. I am proud. When young David killed Goliath, King Saul was glad to get rid of his enemy and honor David; but when David started slaying his ten thousands in contrast to Saul's thousands, then the king became envious and angry. David was poor in spirit: "Who am I? and what is my life, or my father's family in Israel, that I should be son in law to the king?" (1 Samuel 18:18). At no time did David use his position to promote himself; he was willing for God to do the promoting, in His time and in His way. "And David behaved himself wisely in all his ways; and the LORD was with him" (1 Samuel 18:14).

A constant source of friction among the disciples—and it must have grieved their Master's heart—was, "Who is the greatest in the kingdom of heaven?" (Matthew 18:1). Our Lord's answer was to place an unspoiled child in their midst. Why is an unspoiled child great, so much so that men will risk their lives to protect and save him? Because he knows he is a child and acts like a child. When a child starts acting like an adult, he becomes disgusting and offensive. (Perhaps the only thing worse is an adult acting like a child.) But when a child naturally acts like a child, he is a beautiful thing to behold, and you cannot help but love him. A child without guile or affectation is the king! All the world bows before his little throne!

King Saul could not become like a little child and as a result, he lost his crown, his kingdom, and his life. He pretended to be something that he was not. Samuel commanded him to wait for the prophet's arrival before any sacrifices were offered, but Saul could not wait. He pretended to be a priest (1 Samuel 13:5-14), and he impetuously offered the sacrifice. Later, when God gave him another chance and commanded him to exterminate the Amalekites, Saul pretended to be God and deliberately disobeyed the orders (1 Samuel 15). The final scene in Saul's life shows the king completely abandoned by God (1 Samuel 28). He prayed but he got no answers; even the dreams, the priests, and the prophets brought no message from God. So, he decided to consult a witch. "And Saul disguised himself," says 1 Samuel 28:8, and he went by night to a witch's cave. In one sense, Saul did disguise himself; but in another sense, he was revealing his true self! All along he had been rebelling against God, and "rebellion is as the sin of witchcraft" (1 Samuel 15:23). The next day, Saul died a suicide on the field of battle, and his crown was taken by an Amalekite, one of the men Saul himself should have slain (2 Samuel 1:10).

Another evidence of poverty of spirit is *accepting circumstances.* When circumstances do not go my way, do I become angry and critical? Am I always trying to manipulate people and circumstances for my own benefit and comfort? Am I willing to give in to make things easier for somebody else? Do I cut corners and pull deals to accomplish what I want in life? Paul said, "I have learned, in whatsoever state I am, therewith to be content" (Philippians 4:11). This does not mean that Christians never try to improve their circumstances, because that would be complacency, not contentment. But it does mean that the poor in spirit do not chafe in uncomfortable circumstances and spend their time complaining both to God and men.

A third evidence is *a right attitude toward things.* The person who is poor in spirit does not find his satisfaction in things: he can do with or he can do without. "I know both how to be abased, and I know how to abound" (Philippians 4:12). He does not measure a man's worth by how much material wealth the man owns, for "a man's life consisteth not in the abundance of the things which he possesseth" (Luke 12:15). If things change my attitudes, then things are my master, not my servant; and that is the sin of idolatry. The proud man is possessed by things; the humble man possesses things and uses them for the good of others and the glory of God.

The parable of the rich farmer illustrates this truth (Luke 12:13-21). Material wealth is either a window through which we see God or a mirror in which we sees ourselves; and with this farmer, it was the latter. There are eleven personal pronouns in this farmer's conversation with himself! He talks *about* himself *to* himself! And he has no thought for God or his hungry neighbor. Had he been poor in spirit he would have been rich toward God; but because he thought he was rich, he became poor and lost everything. He thought he was an owner, but he discovered (too late) that he was only a steward. God was the Owner, and all the fruits and goods were merely loaned to the man. He possessed, but he did not own.

Thoreau was right when he wrote, "A man is rich in proportion to the number of things which he can afford to let alone." Paul says it better: "For we brought nothing into this world, and it is certain we can carry nothing out. And having food and raiment let us be therewith content" (1 Timothy 6:7-8). The man who is poor in spirit does not build his life on *things*. He has God, and that is all he needs.

Let me suggest a fourth evidence of humility: *accepting God's will for your life.* The person who is poor in spirit joyfully accepts the will of God; the proud person resists God's will. I have met people who are so proud that they even *defy* God. I remember a Christian couple who had big plans for their children and told God what He was supposed to do. Well, He did it, and they lived to regret it. "And he gave them their request; but sent leanness into their soul" (Psalm 106:15).

Sometimes God gives us seeming failure just to teach us to submit to His will. I learned that lesson in a little fishing village in Denmark, where I ministered with a Youth for Christ team back in 1957. I did not know the language, and the people of the village did not seem interested in the Gospel—and I felt like quitting. Very few people were attending the services, but night after night my associate and I led the singing and preached the Word. Before the week ended, we learned that God had indeed changed some hearts—not as many as we had hoped, but far more than we deserved. During that week I learned to obey God's will in spite of my feelings and in spite of the results, a lesson I hope I never forget.

The person who is self-satisfied and self-sufficient, who feels no need for God, is not poor in spirit. The believer who argues with God's will and complains about circumstances is not poor in spirit. The person who fishes for compliments and inflates when the compliments come is not poor in spirit. The leader who is harder on others than he is on himself is not poor in spirit.

To be poor in spirit, then, means to know yourself, accept

yourself, and be yourself, to the glory of God. It means letting God use both your strengths and your weaknesses to accomplish His will and glorify His name.

III

Why does being poor in spirit bring blessing? An attitude of humility is exactly opposite what the world teaches, and usually opposite of what most people practice. "Assert yourself!" is the world's slogan, while Jesus says, "Humble yourself." How can humility bring blessing to you when you live in a cutthroat world?

To begin with, humility is Godlike; and anything that makes us more like God is bound to bring blessing, even if the world will not accept it. "Who is like unto the LORD our God, who dwelleth on high, who humbleth himself to behold the things that are in heaven, and in the earth!" (Psalm 113:5-6). God the Father humbles Himself to behold the things both in heaven and on earth! God the Son "humbled himself, and became obedient unto death, even the death of the cross" (Philippians 2:8). Think of the humility of the Holy Spirit as He lives with us day by day!

It is difficult to conceive of a Christian growing in grace apart from humility. True poverty of Spirit is the soil out of which the fruit of the Spirit can be cultivated. "To this man will I look, even to him that is poor and of a contrite spirit, and trembleth at my word" (Isaiah 66:2). Certainly the seed of God's Word could never be planted in the hard soil of a proud heart. "Break up your fallow ground, and sow not among thorns" (Jeremiah 4:3).

But there is another reason why poverty of spirit brings blessing: it makes us kings. "Blessed are the poor in spirit: for their's is the kingdom of heaven." We control by being controlled. No man has a right to exercise authority who himself is not under authority. We reign in life by submitting to the authority of Jesus Christ (Romans 5:17).

What is involved in reigning in life? It means authority; for when we submit to Christ, He is able to share His authority with us. Pride always weakens a person, because pride cuts us off from fellowship with the Lord. Peter was his weakest when, in pride, he wielded his sword and tried to defend Jesus. Peter was his strongest when he wept bitterly, humbled himself, and submitted to Jesus. Jesus used a little child as the perfect example of a citizen of His Kingdom because in a child you see authority based on humility. Because a child is so weak in himself, he commands all the strength of those about him. The world thinks that authority comes from size, ability, noise, and self-promotion; the Christian knows that true authority comes from poverty of spirit. We reign as kings because we submit as servants.

This spiritual Kingdom not only involves authority, but it also involves liberty. Pride always makes a slave out of a person, while humility sets that person free. When you live to promote yourself, you are bound to become a slave of people or things or circumstances. You are never really free to be yourself, because self has already enslaved you through pride. The person who is poor in spirit is not disturbed by the attitudes or criticisms of others, because he lives to please God. Moses was not afraid of Pharaoh, because Pharaoh could do nothing to hurt God's servant so long as that servant was submitted to the Lord. When you live to promote yourself, you must always get something from others to inflate your ego or advertise your importance; but every time you get something, you pay dearly. "Honor me now, I pray thee, before the elders of my people, and before Israel" pleaded King Saul (1 Samuel 15:30). His pride made him a slave. He was not the king of Israel: Israel was king over him!

Humility means that you look to God for everything you need. This sets you free from people, circumstances, and things. If you need nothing but God, then nothing—and no one—can be a threat to you. You are free!

Humility makes us kings not only by giving us authority and liberty but also by giving us adequacy. "The LORD killeth, and maketh alive: he bringeth down to the grave, and bringeth up. The LORD maketh poor, and maketh rich: he bringeth low, and lifteth up. He raiseth up the poor out of the dust, and lifteth up the beggar out of the dunghill, to set them among princes, and to make them inherit the throne of glory" (1 Samuel 2:6-8). When we are low enough, then God can trust us with a throne and a scepter. He opens the treasures of His grace to the dead, the poor, and the beggars! His feast is spread for "the poor, and the maimed, and the halt, and the blind" (Luke 14:21), not the proud who think their souls can be satisfied with lands, oxen, and honeymoons!

There is a poverty in riches, and there are riches in poverty. "There is that maketh himself rich, yet hath nothing: there is that maketh himself poor, yet hath great riches" (Proverbs 13: 7). "For ye know the grace of our Lord Jesus Christ, that, though he was rich, yet for your sakes he became poor, that ye through his poverty might be rich" (2 Corinthians 8:9). It is a singular fact that the rich people commit suicide while the poor do not. The person who depends on material things cannot reign in life, because he is possessed by the things he possesses. He is controlled by things, and yet he is never satisfied with the things that he has.

When you and I are poor in spirit, God gives us a kingdom, and we reign in life. When King Saul was a humble servant, God gave him a kingdom; but when Saul began to throw his weight around and run things his way, then he lost his kingdom. How did David get his kingdom? By being nobody. This is how Jesus Christ secured His Kingdom: "Wherefore God also hath highly exalted him, and given him a name which is above every name" (Philippians 2:9). This is the paradox of the Christian life: we surrender that we might reign. This leads to authority, liberty, and adequacy.

IV

How can we cultivate this grace of humility? How is it possible to succeed in this difficult world while seeking to be poor in spirit?

I think the first step is to *accept God's estimate of yourself.* You had to do this to become a Christian, and you have to do this to grow in the Christian life. When Christ first confronted you with the Gospel, you perhaps had a difficult time agreeing with His estimate of your life. "For all have sinned, and come short of the glory of God" (Romans 3:23). "There is none righteous, no, not one" (Romans 3:10). "Ye must be born again" (John 3:7). Once you accepted God's estimate of yourself, it was easy to accept God's remedy for your sins. You had to humble yourself, and then God lifted you up.

"For I say, through the grace given unto me, to every man that is among you, not to think of himself more highly than he ought to think; but to think soberly, according as God hath dealt to every man the measure of faith" (Romans 12:3). Paul is not suggesting that we not think of ourselves, because that would be impossible. He is warning us not to think more highly of ourselves than we ought to; and I think we ought to include *less* highly, as well. There is a false humility that degrades as much as does a proud spirit. I suggested early in this chapter that true humility means knowing myself, accepting myself, and being myself, to the glory of God. This means accepting God's estimate of me on the basis of the gifts and the faith He has given me.

For example, Moses argued with God when God called him to go to Egypt. Moses used every excuse he could find, all of them centered in his own weaknesses. Gideon made the same mistake when God called him to deliver the people from the power of Midian. Imagine God calling a fearful farmer a "mighty man of valour" (Judges 6:12)! Imagine Jesus Christ calling Simon a "rock" (Matthew 16:18)! When Moses, Gideon, and Simon accepted God's estimate and acted upon it by faith, they accomplished great things for God. They found their kingdom by humbly yielding to God and daring to believe what He said. Every victory they won was the result of their faith in God's Word.

As you read your Bible, notice what God says about you as a child of God. Accept what He says, and act upon it. When Moses, Gideon, and Peter argued with the Word of God, it led to defeat. When they accepted the Word and acted upon it, it led to victory. God does not say to us, "Obey, and I will bless you." Rather, He says, "I have already blessed you with all spiritual blessings in Christ (Ephesians 1:3); now, draw upon this wealth, believe what I say, and live like a king!"

The second step is to *yield yourself to God daily,* and draw your strength from Him. "Without me, ye can do nothing" (John 15:5). Many Christians find it helpful to get up early enough in the morning to spend time uninterrupted in prayer and meditation on God's Word. What digestion is to your body, meditation is to your soul; and what food is to digestion, the Word of God is to meditation. "Man shall not live by bread alone, but by every word that proceedeth out of the mouth of God" (Matthew 4:4). The Word of God taken into your inner man releases power. The Bible is the scepter by which you reign in life. Spend time daily in quiet communion with God, and carry the power of that experience with you all through the day. We do not read that King Saul was a great man of prayer, or that he meditated on the Word; but in the Psalms, we constantly meet King David talking to God and letting God talk to him.

The Word of God will transform your mind (Romans 12:2) so that you will have "the mind of Christ"—the same attitude Jesus had when He laid aside His glory and came to earth as a servant (Philippians 2:5-7). You were not born with the attitude of a servant; you were born with the attitude of a rebel. It is only as the mind is transformed by the Word that we can ever cultivate true humility and poverty of spirit.

The third step is this: *focus on Christ and His blessings.* Too many people think that humility comes from studying their own sins and failures, but this is not true. It is not the badness of man that leads to repentance, but "the goodness of God" (Romans 2:4). If you conduct too many spiritual "autopsies," you may bleed to death! There is nothing wrong with honest self-examination *provided that you look to Christ.* However, too many Christians spend too much time looking into the mirror when they ought to be "looking unto Jesus, the author and finisher of our faith" (Hebrews 12:2). The more you contemplate the goodness of God, the lower you will sink before Him. "Who am I, O LORD God, and what is mine house, that thou hast brought me hitherto?" (1 Chronicles 17:16) prayed King David; but you will never find King Saul praying like that.

Peter's experience with the Lord in Luke 5 is a good illustration of the truth that humility comes from contemplating God's blessings and not our own failures. Peter had fished all night and caught nothing, when Jesus entered his boat and used it for a platform as He taught the multitudes. Peter was a captive audience and had to listen to the Word; but this Word was preparing him for a miracle. ("Faith cometh by hearing, and hearing by the Word of God" [Romans 10:17].) When Jesus commanded Peter to launch out into the deep, the fisherman protested weakly but obeyed; and the result was a great catch of fish. "When Simon Peter saw it, he fell down at Jesus' knees, saying, Depart from me; for I am a sinful man, O Lord!" (v. 8). It was not his night of failure that drove Peter to his knees but the great success that Jesus gave to him! Anybody can say "I am a sinful man!" when he has failed; but it takes an honest, humble man to say this when he has succeeded. It was the goodness of God that led Peter to repentance; and if you and I will only meditate on His goodness, we, too, will grow in humility and poverty of spirit.

Let me suggest a fourth step: *look for opportunities to serve others.* Humility and service go together. The proud man looks for others to serve him, while the humble man looks for ways to serve others. "Let each esteem other better than themselves" (Philippians 2:3). "By love serve one another" (Galatians 5:13). "Yea, and if I be offered upon the sacrifice and service of your faith, I joy, and rejoice with you all" (Philippians 2: 17). Sacrifice and service are the twin children of humility. It is important to note that this sacrifice and service must go unnoticed and unrewarded. "They have their reward!" If we blow a trumpet every time we help somebody, we will only nourish our pride and starve our humility. A cup of cold water for Jesus' sake is all that He asks.

Do not look for *big* opportunities, "worthy" of your abilities. Those will come in due time. The great saints of the Bible started as servants, not rulers; and they were faithful over a few things before God made them kings. Moses tended sheep; Joseph was a steward; David was a shepherd; even Jesus was a carpenter. Live with the eye of God upon you, and forget the praise of men. Serve faithfully in the hidden place, and in due time, God will lift you up. Every opportunity for service is an opportunity to exercise sovereignty in Christ. We reign in life by living to serve, to the glory of God.

The sin of pride has ruined more lives than perhaps any other sin. It is the sin that invites Satan to rule. It is the sin that cost King Saul his character, his crown, and, ultimately, his life. Humility is the grace that made David a king!

"Blessed are the poor in spirit: for their's is the kingdom of heaven."

Blessed are they that mourn: for they shall be comforted.

Matthew 5:4

For godly sorrow worketh repentance to salvation not to be repented of: but the sorrow of the world worketh death.

2 Corinthians 7:10

And Peter went out, and wept bitterly.

Luke 22:62

And he [Judas] cast down the pieces of silver in the temple, and departed, and went and hanged himself.

Matthew 27:5

As sorrowful, yet always rejoicing.

2 Corinthians 6:10

He hath sent me to bind up the brokenhearted . . . to comfort all that mourn.

Isaiah 61:1-2

Weeping may endure for a night, but joy cometh in the morning.

Psalm 30:5

4

The Mourners

IF YOU WANT TO KNOW a person's character, find out what makes him laugh and what makes him weep. This test is not infallible, because we all have our difficult days; but generally speaking, it is true. It always amazes me when people laugh at a drunk or at a comedian impersonating a drunk. I see nothing funny in drunkenness or in drunken behavior. As a pastor, I have seen too much of the tragedy of drink to be entertained by a drunk.

What we laugh at and what we weep over indicate our values of life, and values are a part of maturity. Little children will laugh at things that seem stupid to us, and they will cry over matters that seem trivial to us. I read about a terrible train accident in Great Britain that killed a number of passengers. In one of the cars was a mother with a little child in her arms, and the mother was dead but the child was unharmed. When the rescuers took the child away from the dead mother, the child laughed and played; but when they took away her candy, she broke into a terrible tantrum of weeping and screaming. The fact that her mother was dead did not bother the child, because she knew nothing about death. But she did know about candy!

This means that the higher you go in life, the more vulnerable you are to sorrow. You can escape sorrow if you wish to, simply by isolating yourself from other people and from the affairs of life; but at the same time you will also be escaping joy. For the higher you go in the scale of life, the greater the opportunities for joy; and the same things that cause joy can

45

also cause sorrow. Animals feel pain, and some pets seem to show sorrow; but for the most part, animals know nothing of a broken heart. But how many of us are willing to become animals just to avoid sorrow? Most children know nothing of the deep hurts that bring tears to adult eyes; but how many of us would want to become children just to escape the pains of adult life?

Whenever you enter into the experience of joy, you make yourself a candidate for sorrow. A young couple that marries experiences joy; but suppose she comes down with a terminal illness, or suppose he is hopelessly crippled in an accident? A couple can bring children into the world, and children are a joy; but suppose one of them develops leukemia and dies? Just about everything in life that brings joy can also be a source of sorrow; and the only way to escape that sorrow is to run away from life.

Jesus never tried to escape the sorrows of life. Nor did He deny that they existed. *He transformed them.* Jesus did not tell His disciples to go out and look for sorrow; but He did tell them that He was able to transform their tears and bring them comfort. Of itself, sorrow never makes a person better. I have seen it make people bitter. But sorrow plus Jesus Christ can bring a transforming experience of power into the life of the one who is mourning.

If you and I are to experience the comfort of God, we must understand the three different kinds of sorrow that can come to us in life.

I

First, there is *natural* sorrow. This kind of sorrow comes to everybody—saved and unsaved, rich and poor, young and old. It is a natural part of life. God made us to be able to weep. Some of the songs and sermons you hear give the impression that a Christian never weeps, that the Christian life is a constant song in the sunshine. But Abraham, the great man of faith, wept when his dear wife died; and David wept when his rebellious son was killed in battle. Jeremiah wept when he saw his beloved nation go into captivity. Jesus wept over the lost city of Jerusalem; He also wept at the tomb of His friend Lazarus. Jesus never wept for Himself; and He admonished the women of Jerusalem not to weep over Him; but He did weep for others. When Paul said farewell to his dear friends from Ephesus, he wept, and they wept. As you read the Bible, you get the impression that God expects His people to weep. "To every thing there is a season, and a time to every purpose under the heaven: a time to be born, and a time to die . . . a time to weep, and a time to laugh" (Ecclesiastes 3:1-2, 4).

When God created the first man, He gave him the ability to weep; and He did this *before* man had sinned. Natural weeping is not sinful. On the contrary, it is a gift from God. There is healing in natural weeping. Doctors and psychologists in the past twenty-five years have helped us to understand what really happens when we mourn, and their discoveries have helped us (with God's assistance) to heal the brokenhearted. Natural sorrow expressed in mourning releases a healing process in a person's life that enables him to accept the pain, work his way through it, and adjust to life again. In my ministry I have noticed that the people who, for one reason or another, do not mourn, do not easily adjust to new circumstances; the wound never seems to heal.

Mourning is an expression of love. It is also a proof that the person has accepted the fact of death (or whatever the crisis might be) and wants to handle it in an adult way. When the pain is kept inside, it seems to poison the emotional system, the way an infection spreads through the bloodstream. I have heard well-meaning people say in funeral homes, "Now, don't cry! You know she is better off!" Don't cry! Why, the thing the person needs to do more than anything else is to cry! This is God's way of helping him release the pressure and pain inside, and it is a perfectly natural thing. Some people have the idea that weeping is a sign of weakness. Self-pity is a sign of weakness, but not weeping. Jesus was the strongest Man who ever walked on this earth, and He wept openly!

There is a hopeless sorrow that people experience who do not know Christ. "I would not have you to be ignorant, brethren, concerning them which are asleep, that ye sorrow not, even as others which have no hope" (1 Thessalonians 4:13). Paul goes on to explain why the Christian has hope even while he is weeping. To begin with, for the Christian death is sleep; the body goes to sleep, and the soul goes home to God. One day Christ will return and will bring with Him those who have died in Christ and gone on before us; and we shall "ever be with the Lord" (v. 17). When a Christian loved one or friend dies, and we weep, our mourning is certainly not for the loved one but for ourselves. Death is like an amputation, and the closer we are in life, the harder it is in death. But our sorrow need not be hopeless, because we have eternal hope in Jesus Christ and in the promises of His Word.

II

The second kind of sorrow is *unnatural* sorrow. It is unnatural because its effects in our lives are opposite what God wants us to experience. Godly sorrow heals, but unnatural sorrow makes the wounds deeper and fills the heart with pain. Natural sorrow gradually helps us put life back together again, but unnatural sorrow tears things apart and keeps them that way. When you sorrow in a natural way, you learn to face and accept reality; but unnatural sorrow isolates you from reality and makes it difficult for you to adjust to the demands of life. I have known people who have grieved themselves into physical affliction and even mental unbalance. True sorrow enables us to experience the comfort of God; but unnatural sorrow blinds us to God's comfort and seems to give us, instead, the condemnation of God: there is a growing feeling of guilt instead of an experience of grace. Natural sorrow enables us to remember the lost loved one and use those memories constructively; but unnatural sorrow turns memories into punishments that destroy the peace and balance that God wants us to have.

Psychologists who have studied bereavement tell us that unnatural sorrow can have many causes. One major cause is selfishness. A self-centered person uses other people—even the closest loved ones—to make his own life safe and pleasant; and if he loses a loved one, it upsets his life-style, and it hurts. His tears are more for himself than for the deceased. Fear is another cause of unnatural sorrow—fear of the future, fear of change, perhaps even fear of death itself. Excessive tears and mourning then become an invisible armor to protect the person from the hard knocks of life. He is saying, "Don't lay any responsibility on me! Don't demand too much of me! Can't you see I have enough to bear already?"

But perhaps the greatest cause of unnatural grief is guilt: it is our way of atoning for past failures and sins in connection with the deceased. Some people atone for their sins by purchasing expensive, elaborate funerals. I recall one lady who took her life's savings—all that she had—and bought her husband the most expensive casket available. She put her financial future into the grave with him, but it was her way of saying to him, "Dear, I'm sorry for the mean things I said and did while you were sick." I think of another man who visited his wife's grave almost every day for months after her death, no matter what the weather was, not as a sign of love but as a work of atonement. It reminded me of the great Samuel Johnson, who stood in the rain with his head uncovered to atone for a boyish act of disobedience to his father.

King David illustrates this unnatural sorrow that is caused by guilt. You will recall that David's disobedient son Absalom tried to take the kingdom away from him, and almost succeeded (2 Samuel 15-20). We get the impression that Absalom was a favored, pampered son; certainly he was a vain fellow who was proud of his beauty, especially his hair (2 Samuel 14:25-26). He secretly plotted against his father, drove David from Jerusalem, took over the palace, and then planned to attack David's

divided forces and utterly wipe them out. Instead, David won
the battle and Absalom was slain, a judgment the young man
certainly deserved. Before the battle, David begged his leaders,
"Deal gently for my sake with the young man, even with Absalom" (2 Samuel 18:5). When David received the tragic news
that Absalom had been slain, he expressed his sorrow in words
that have become familiar: "O my son Absalom, my son, my
son Absalom! Would God I had died for thee, O Absalom,
my son, my son!" (2 Samuel 18:33). While we admire David's
love, we question his thinking. Would it have been better for
the nation for David to die and for rebellious Absalom to live?

There is no doubt that Absalom's death was part of the pay-
ment that David made because of his adultery with Bathsheba.
When confronted with the sin of "the rich man" who stole the
little ewe lamb—a picture of David himself—the king said,
"As the LORD liveth, the man that hath done this thing shall
surely die: and he shall restore the lamb fourfold, because he
did this thing, and because he had no pity" (2 Samuel 12:5-6).
David did restore fourfold: the baby died, his daughter Tamar
was violated, his son Amnon was slain, and Absalom was slain.
Because David temporarily lost control of himself, he temporarily lost the rule over his kingdom. It was a great price to
pay for a few moments of pleasure.

But David's mourning over Absalom was not natural. Second Samuel 19 tells us that the soldiers were actually ashamed
of their victory because it brought such sorrow to their king!
David refused to be comforted. Why? Because he was atoning
for his sins. It took the blunt speech of Joab to show the king
how selfish he was. "I perceive," said Joab, "that if Absalom
had lived, and all we had died this day, then it had pleased thee
well" (2 Samuel 19:6). David's abnormal grief had so isolated
him from reality that he was unable to live like a king and rule
over himself and his people.

The sorrows of life do not *create* problems, they *reveal* them.
Absalom's death and David's unnatural mourning revealed to
the world that David had not been in control of his own family

and that his own sins had found him out. Instead of trying to atone for his sin, David should have trusted God for the forgiveness that he needed. This is what he did when he confessed his sin of adultery, and God graciously forgave him. "For thou desirest not sacrifice; else would I give it: thou delightest not in burnt-offering. The sacrifices of God are a broken spirit: a broken and a contrite heart, O God, thou wilt not despise" (Psalm 51:16-17).

We, today, do not bring bulls and goats; we bring excessive tears as our sacrifices. Yet God wants neither one! The comfort of God comes to those who trust the grace of God, not to those who try to earn God's comfort by unnatural sorrow. Even though our sorrows may be caused by our sins, as were David's, we can still confess those sins to the Lord, claim His forgiveness, and experience His comfort. Absalom almost stole the kingdom from David, but David almost lost it by his own foolishness! When you reign in life it means you have control over your own emotions; when you give way to unnatural sorrow, you get off the throne and lose control of life.

III

But the main thrust of this beatitude is *supernatural* sorrow. Jesus is talking about repentance for sin, and that is the result of the supernatural working of God in your life. "For godly sorrow worketh repentance to salvation not to be repented of: but the sorrow of the world worketh death" (2 Corinthians 7:10).

This godly sorrow is the logical result of the experience of the first beatitude: "Blessed are the poor in spirit: for their's is the kingdom of heaven." When a person sees his spiritual bankruptcy, he can respond in one of four ways. He can deny that this bankruptcy exists and, like the Pharisees, put on a front. But this leads to a life of deception in which the person uses most of his strength to pretend, so that he has little energy left for living. Second, he can admit his spiritual bankruptcy and try to change things himself. But this is a case of the poor helping the poor! Third, he can admit his need and so despair over it that he gives up completely. This is "the sorrow of the world" that produces death. Judas saw what a sinner he was and went out and committed suicide. Peter saw what a sinner he was and went out and wept bitterly. That is the difference between the sorrow of the world and the godly sorrow that leads to repentance. The logical thing for a person to do when he sees his own spiritual need is to admit it and then *turn to God for what he needs.* The person who is sincerely poor in spirit will mourn over himself and his sins, and through this mourning he will experience the comfort of God.

We must distinguish, however, between repentance and remorse and regret. When my consciousness of sin rests only in my mind, then it is regret. When it affects my mind and my heart, it is remorse and remorse is a dangerous thing. But when my concern over my sin brings me to the place where I am willing to turn from it and obey God—when my concern affects my *will* as well as my mind and my heart—then I have experienced true repentance.

You may remember the story about the Sunday school teacher who asked a pupil to define repentance, and the boy replied: "Repentance means sorrow for sin." "That's right!" said the teacher. But then a little girl spoke up: "Excuse me, but it means being sorry enough to quit!' She knew that repentance involves not only a change in feeling and thinking but also a change in *willing.* If a person truly changes his mind about sin, he will act differently.

The prodigal son (Luke 15) illustrates the truth perfectly; his mind, heart, and will were all involved in his repentance. His mind told him that his father's servants were better off than he was; his heart made him sick of his situation—"I perish with hunger!"—and his will motivated him to arise and go to his father. Had he sat there in the pigpen thinking how foolish he had been, it would have been regret. Had he thought about his sins and hated himself for committing them, it would have been remorse. When he said, "I will arise and go!"—and he arose and went—that was repentance. His sorrow was a godly sorrow that motivated him to return home and experience forgiveness.

<h2 style="text-align:center">IV</h2>

About what are we supposed to repent? Obviously, we should repent of our sins. "For I will declare my iniquity; I will be sorry for my sin" (Psalm 38:18). We must be careful that it is *sin* over which we sorrow, and not the painful consequences of sin or the fact that we have been caught. Too many people fail to see the difference. When the sinner repents of his sins and puts his faith in Jesus Christ, then he is saved. This was Paul's message: "repentance toward God, and faith toward our Lord Jesus Christ" (Acts 20:21).

Does God expect His own children to repent? I think that He does. Paul commended the believers at Corinth because they received his letter and "sorrowed to repentance" (2 Corinthians 7:9). On the other hand, Paul warned that same church that he would come and discipline those who had not repented, and certainly he was talking about professed Christians (2 Corinthians 12:21). In His last message to the Church, our Lord commands His people to repent (Revelation 2:5, 16; 3:3, 19).

We must beware of an easy and comfortable dealing with our sins. It was this surface dealing with sin that cost King Saul his crown. The record is in 1 Samuel 15. First, Saul lied about his sin: "I have performed the commandment of the LORD" (v. 13). Then, he made an excuse instead of a confession: it was "the people" who had disobeyed God, not Saul! Finally, Saul used religion to defend sin! He said he would use the animals that were spared as sacrifices for the Lord! Even after Samuel exposed Saul's wickedness, the king persisted in defending himself and blaming the people (vv. 20-21). And when King Saul finally said, "I have sinned," (v. 30), he still qualified his confession with a condition: "Yet honor me now, I pray thee, before the elders of my people, and before Israel" (v. 30).

He was more concerned about his reputation than his character, what men thought than what God thought.

From that point on, Saul began to lose his kingdom, and David began to gain his kingdom. It was David, not Saul, who defeated Goliath (1 Samuel 17). David slew tens of thousands of the enemy, while Saul slew only his thousands (1 Samuel 18:7). Saul began to fear and suspect; he tried to kill David; he even turned against Jonathan, his own son. God departed from Saul, and the record closes with King Saul turning to Satan for help as he inquired of a witch (1 Samuel 28), and then dying in shame on the field of battle. Nothing leads to defeat in the Christian life like a surface dealing with sin.

This does not mean that the disobedient believer must wallow in self-reproach and condemnation, because even that attitude could be sinful. Paul told the Corinthians to forgive the man who had been guilty of sin "lest perhaps such a one should be swallowed up with overmuch sorrow" (2 Corinthians 2:7). Why? "Lest Satan should get an advantage of us" (2 Corinthians 2:11). Satan is the "accuser of the brethren" (Revelation 12:10); he likes nothing better than to remind the saints of their sins and make them miserable to the point of giving up.

There are two extremes to avoid when it comes to dealing with our sins: being too easy on ourselves and being too hard on ourselves. Either extreme will cost us the enjoyment of our kingdom. King Saul was too easy on his sins and he lost the crown; and David was too hard on himself at the death of Absalom, and he almost lost the crown.

Yes, as Christians we must repent of our sins. This means more than admitting them and trying to explain or excuse them. It means admitting them, looking upon them the way God does, abhorring them, and turning from them. "A broken and a contrite heart, O God, thou wilt not despise" (Psalm 51:17). Simply quoting 1 John 1:9 in a glib manner is not true repentance. That promise is not an excuse for sin; it is an encouragement to believers who want to get rid of sin. "If we confess our sins, he is faithful and just to forgive us our sins, and to cleanse us from all unrighteousness." That word "confess" literally means "to say the same thing." If I am to be forgiven, I must agree with God's verdict about my sins. King Saul said, "I have sinned" and then proceeded to argue with the prophet and make excuses. King David said, "I have sinned" and the prophet said to him, "The LORD also hath put away thy sin; thou shalt not die" (2 Samuel 12:13).

It is necessary for us to repent of our sins, but this is only the beginning. Anyone can mourn over his sins, but not too many people mourn over the very fact that they are sinners. We should show sorrow not only for what we do but for what we are. This kind of sorrow seems strange to the superficial Christian; but it was not strange to the godly men and women of the Bible and the saints of church history. "Behold, I was shapen in iniquity; and in sin did my mother conceive me" (Psalm 51:5) was not David's excuse for his disobedience. It was his expression of a deeper repentance. "I am not only sorry for what I did, but I am also sorry for what I am." As you read Psalm 51, you realize that David was confessing the fact that his very being was polluted by sin. His "inward parts" were defiled (v. 6); his ears no longer heard joy (v. 8); his heart was dirty, and his spirit needed renewal (v. 10); even his tongue and his lips were paralyzed by sin (vv. 14-15)! His eyes saw nothing but sin: "my sin is ever before me" (v. 3). Here is a man who repented of his sins, but not in a superficial way: he exposed every part of his being to the holy searchlight of God.

But this mourning goes even deeper. We repent not only of what we do and what we are, but we also mourn over what sin does in this world. Jeremiah wept over the sins of his people, Jesus wept over the sins of Jerusalem, Paul wept as he ministered in the churches. All of creation is groaning because of sin, and the believer joins in that groaning (Romans 8:22-23). While we thank God that He gives to us in this world "richly all things to enjoy" (1 Timothy 6:17), we also weep because our

Father's world has been so polluted and plundered by sin. The present crisis in ecology is but a symptom of that deeper crisis. Many people weep over the loss of precious resources and the marring of irreplaceable beauty, but few weep over the godless rebellion in man's heart that has caused this crisis.

We not only mourn over sin in our lives and in the world God made, but we also mourn over sin in the lives of others. When a member of the church at Corinth was living in shameless incest, the church members should have mourned; but instead, they boasted of their open-mindedness! (Read 1 Corinthians 5.) "And ye are puffed up, and have not rather mourned," scolds Paul (v. 2). The Greek word translated "mourned" means "to mourn as for the dead." If the believers at Corinth had truly mourned because of this sin, they would have lovingly dealt with the offender and brought him to a place of repentance. "Brethren, if a man be overtaken in a fault, ye which are spiritual, restore such an one in the spirit of meekness" (Galatians 6:1).

The Christian who is able to deal with sin in his own life can be trusted to deal with sin in the lives of others. He will be neither too easy nor too hard. It is often the case that those who are too easy on themselves will be hard on others. Saul excused himself for disobeying God, yet he threatened to kill his son Jonathan for disobeying his (Saul's) foolish commandment (1 Samuel 14:24-45). David was excessively hard on himself and yet too easy on Absalom. Maintaining a balance in dealing with sin—our own and others'—requires the wisdom of God and the leading of His Spirit. Satan welcomes either extreme. If we are too easy in dealing with sin, the matter is not settled to the glory of God; if we are too hard, it could result in "overmuch sorrow" and defeat.

It may seem strange, but this mourning over sin can go even deeper. We mourn over what we do, what we are, and what sin has wrought in this world and in the lives of others; but we also mourn over our mourning. This may sound neurotic, but it is not. As we grow in grace, we realize more and more how inadequate we are to face God and deal with our sins. Jeremiah was not satisfied with his mourning. "Oh that my head were waters, and mine eyes a fountain of tears, that I might weep day and night for the slain of the daughter of my people!" (Jeremiah 9:1). "For these things I weep; mine eye, mine eye runneth down with water" (Lamentations 1:16). As you read his Lamentations, you realize how deeply his heart was moved because of sin; and the sin was not even his own!

When you and I learn how to mourn, then we will have a deeper understanding of the sinfulness of sin and the graciousness of God.

V

Christ promises comfort to those who mourn, but what kind of comfort is it? You can be sure that it is far deeper than sympathy, the drying of the tears and the enfolding of the child in the arms of love. Our English word *comfort* comes from two Latin words that mean "with strength." (The words *fortify* and *fortress* carry the same meaning.) We are prone to confuse *comfort* and *sympathy,* but they are not identical. To sympathize means "to feel with," while to comfort means "to encourage, to give strength." Our mourning puts us in touch with the eternal resources of God, and the result is God's comfort. "In the day when I cried thou answeredst me, and strengthenedst me with strength in my soul" (Psalm 138:3).

Our God is the "God of all comfort" (2 Corinthians 1:3). His attitude toward us is not one of hostility, but one of love and encouragement. He is not against us; He is *for* us. This is one of the emphases in Romans 8. The Holy Spirit makes intercession for us (v. 26). God the Father delivered up His Son for us (v. 32). God the Son is making intercession for us (v. 34). No wonder Paul cries, "If God be for us, who can be against us?" (v. 31). " 'For I know the plans that I have for you,' declares the LORD, 'plans for welfare and not for calamity to give you a future and a hope' " (Jeremiah 29:11 NASB). Our comfort and encouragement is God Himself. "But David encouraged himself in the LORD his God" (1 Samuel 30:6). How different from King Saul, who refused to mourn over his sin. "Then Saul fell straightway all along on the earth, and was sore afraid" (1 Samuel 28:20).

There is also the comfort of the Scriptures. "For whatsoever things were written aforetime were written for our learning, that we through patience and comfort of the scriptures might have hope. Now the God of patience and consolation grant you to be likeminded toward one another according to Christ Jesus" (Romans 15:4-5). The same Word that reveals our sins also reveals the grace and forgiveness of God. Nathan said to David, "Thou art the man!" (2 Samuel 12:7). But he also said, "The LORD also hath put away thy sin" (v. 13). The sinful woman mourned at Jesus' feet, and He said to her, "Thy sins are forgiven. . . . Thy faith hath saved thee; go in peace" (Luke 7:48, 50). To the woman taken in the act of adultery He said, "Neither do I condemn thee: go, and sin no more" (John 8:11).

But God also gives us the comfort of the Holy Spirit, for the Spirit is the Comforter (John 14:16). He is the great Encourager, the One who puts strength in our souls. In the Scriptures, we have the *objective* source of comfort; and in the Spirit within, we have the *subjective* source of comfort. The same Spirit who wrote the Word lives in our hearts, and He opens up the Scriptures so that His comfort comes into our lives. Only those who have experienced the comforting ministry of the Holy Spirit can understand this holy experience.

Finally, God comforts us through His people. Often the Holy Spirit uses another Christian to bring us the encouragement that we need. God comforted Paul by the coming of Titus (2 Corinthians 7:6), and Titus comforted Paul by reporting that the problems in the church were being solved. In fact, one reason that Christians go through difficulties is that we might be able to experience the comfort of God and then share that comfort with others. God "comforteth us in all our tribulation, that we may be able to comfort them which are in any trouble, by the comfort wherewith we ourselves are comforted of God" (2 Corinthians 1:4). This does not mean that we must experience exactly the same trial to be of encouragement to others, because God's comfort enables us to encourage those who are in "any trouble." God's comfort is not a luxury for us to hoard; it is a necessity that we must share. "Bear ye one another's burdens, and so fulfil the law of Christ" (Galatians 6:2).

VI

Our Lord was "a man of sorrows, and acquainted with grief" (Isaiah 53:3). He knew what it was to mourn, not over His own sins, of course, because He had no sin (2 Corinthians 5:21), but over the sins of the world and the havoc sin has wrought in the world. He wept at the tomb of Lazarus even though He knew He would raise Lazarus from the dead. In the garden, Jesus wept "with strong crying and tears" (Hebrews 5:7) as He faced the cross, knowing that the eternal sorrow for sin would come up on Him there. What a paradox that He should suffer such great sorrow while at the same time looking to "the joy that was set before him" (Hebrews 12:2).

That Jesus Christ was the Man of sorrows suggests that, as we experience true mourning for sin, we become more like Christ. It is significant that the people thought that Jesus was Jeremiah returned from the grave (Matthew 16:14), because Jeremiah, too, was a man of sorrows and acquainted with grief. "Is it nothing to you, all ye that pass by? behold, and see if there be any sorrow like unto my sorrow" (Lamentations 1:12). Of course, we must not major in mourning; there is also the "joy of the Lord" which is our strength (Nehemiah 8:10). But as we pray, we see ourselves (as did Abraham) "but dust and ashes" (Genesis 18:27). As we see God's blessing, we confess with Peter: "Depart from me; for I am a sinful man, O Lord" (Luke 5:8). There is always new mourning, and there is always new comfort; and this process makes us more like the Master.

The tears of the believer work *for* him and are an investment in future joys. Not all of our comfort will be given today. "Weeping may endure for a night, but joy cometh in the morning" (Psalm 30:5). "They that sow in tears shall reap in joy" (Psalm 126:5). "And God shall wipe away all tears from their eyes" (Revelation 21:4). Psalm 56:8 teaches us that none of our tears will go unnoticed by God: "Put thou my tears into thy bottle: are they not in thy book?" If God sees the sparrow fall, will He not also see our tears fall? Heaven will be a place of no tears, but hell will be a place of nothing but tears. It was Jesus who said, "There shall be weeping and gnashing of teeth" (Matthew 8:12).

There is one way that the believer will never become like the Man of sorrows: He never wept for Himself; He always wept for others. He said to the sympathetic women of Jerusalem, "Weep not for me, but weep for yourselves, and for your children" (Luke 23:28). Until we see Him in glory and become like Him, we will have to weep for ourselves. "Not as though I had already attained, either were already perfect" (Philippians 3:12). But as we weep, we can be sure of His promise: "Blessed are they that mourn: for they shall be comforted."

Blessed are the meek: for they shall inherit the earth.

Matthew 5:5

Take my yoke upon you, and learn of me; for I am meek and lowly in heart: and ye shall find rest unto your souls.

Matthew 11:29

Now the man Moses was very meek, above all the men which were upon the face of the earth.

Numbers 12:3

The fruit of the Spirit is . . . meekness.

Galatians 5:22-23

With all lowliness and meekness, with longsuffering, forbearing one another in love.

Ephesians 4:2

Receive with meekness the engrafted word.

James 1:21

5

The Meek

LET'S BEGIN with the meaning of meekness. Most people have the idea that meekness is weakness. We live in a world that worships power and that rejects any evidence of weakness; and perhaps this explains why many successful people will have little or nothing to do with the Christian faith. They have heard about "Gentle Jesus meek and mild," and they want nothing to do with Him. The ladder of success in today's world is climbed with heavy steps; there is no place for the slippers of timidity.

But meekness is not weakness or timidity. Meekness is power under control. Certainly nobody could accuse Moses of being a weak, timid man; yet God identified him as the meekest man on the face of the earth. Jesus was the most courageous man ever to walk among men, and yet He said, "I am meek and lowly in heart" (Matthew 11:29). Both Moses and Jesus faced difficult, dangerous situations and came through victoriously because they exercised power under control.

God has given us the ability to become angry. Nowhere does the Bible honor the spineless person who is unable (or unwilling) to exercise the right kind of anger. "Be ye angry, and sin not" (Ephesians 4:26). There is a sinless anger, such as when Moses came down from Sinai and saw his people revelling in sin or when Jesus strode into the Temple and majestically cleansed His Father's house. There is a godless anger that destroys, but there is a godly anger that builds up. Two verses from Proverbs explain the difference: "He that is slow to anger is better than the mighty; and he that ruleth his spirit than he that taketh a city" (Proverbs 16:32). That is power under control. "He that hath no rule over his own spirit is like a city that is broken down, and without walls" (Proverbs 25:28). That is power out of control.

Someone has said, "Temper is such a wonderful thing that it's a shame to lose it!" We temper steel to make it stronger. The person who loses his temper loses control of himself and stops living like a king. A successful businessman, Roger Babson, once said, "The best administrator is the governor of his temper."

"Anyone can become angry," wrote Aristotle in his *Nicomachean Ethics,* "that is easy. But to be angry with the right person, to the right degree, at the right time, for the right purpose, and in the right way—this is not easy." What the great philosopher was talking about is meekness—power under control. Anger is power, just as fire is power. (We sometimes say, "His anger flared up!") When fire is under control, it is our servant and accomplishes great things for us; but when fire is out of control, it becomes our master, and the result is destruction. So it is with anger.

"There's nothing wrong with losing my temper," a lady once told evangelist Billy Sunday. "I blow up, and then it's over with."

"So does a shotgun," the evangelist replied, "but look at the damage that's left behind."

The Greek word that is translated *meekness* was a familiar word to the people back in Jesus' day. It was used to describe a soothing medicine. Here is a patient wrestling with a fever, and the doctor gives him medication that quiets him down and relieves the burning so the patient can sleep. The word also was used to describe a gentle breeze. Have you ever been exhausted on a hot day and then felt a cooling breeze blow upon your body? How refreshing it is! But the doctors and the sailors were not the only ones to use this word, because the farmers used it, too. It was used to describe a colt that had been broken. Every colt has to be broken, or it cannot fulfill its function on the farm. Somebody has to break the colt so that its power can be channeled into constructive work.

Now, look at these three illustrations: medicine, wind, and a colt. What do they all have in common? Power! Medicine has power to work in the body to calm nerves, kill germs, strengthen organs, and promote healing. Certainly the wind has power. In 1965, "Hurricane Betsy" did over a billion dollars' damage and cost insurance companies $750 million in claims. That is power! If you have ever watched a cowboy on a bucking bronco, you know that a horse is a powerful animal. But the medicine, wind, and horse must keep the power under control, otherwise they will do damage. The proper dosage of medicine can promote healing, but an overdose may kill. A summer breeze is a delightful thing, but a hurricane only destroys. A broken horse can give both work and pleasure to his master, but a horse out of control is a dangerous thing. All of these have power, and when that power is under control, it is called meekness.

II

Perhaps the best way to understand meekness is to see it at work in the lives of people like ourselves.

When Abraham left Ur of the Chaldees, he took his nephew Lot with him, and it was not long before there was a family disagreement. The story is recorded in Genesis 13. "And there was a strife between the herdmen of Abram's cattle and the herdmen of Lot's cattle" (v. 7). If you were Abraham, what would you have done? Certainly Abraham had the authority to tell Lot to pack up and get moving! After all, Abraham was God's chosen servant; he was even called "the friend of God." It was Abraham that God called and with whom God had made his covenant; Lot was simply a hitchhiker. Abraham had power over Lot, but he kept that power under control. He exercised meekness. Read the story:

> And Abram said unto Lot, Let there be no strife, I pray thee, between me and thee, and between my herdmen and thy herdmen; for we be brethren. Is not the whole land before thee? separate thyself, I pray thee, from me: if thou wilt take the left hand, then I will go to the right; or if thou depart to the right hand, then I will go to the left (Genesis 13:8-9).

Had Abraham been like most of us, he would have said, "I am the elder in this clan, and I get first choice!" To many people, that kind of an attitude would have been "exercising leadership." To God, it would have been committing sin. Abraham had power, but his power was under control, and he gave Lot first choice. "In honor preferring one another" (Romans 12:10). "Let each esteem others more important than themselves" (Philippians 2:3, literal translation). Because Abraham was surrendered to God, he was not afraid to submit to Lot. Abraham knew that his own inheritance was secure in the Lord and that no decision on the part of his nephew could ever rob him of anything that God had for him. Abraham had power, but his power was under control; so God kept His promise and enabled Abraham to "inherit the earth."

Joseph is another vivid illustration of meekness. Mistreated by his brothers, Joseph was sold into Egypt as a slave. Lied about by his master's wife, he was put into prison. But one day, Joseph was elevated to become the prime minister of Egypt. He had the power to revenge himself on his master's wife, but there is no record that he did it. And then his brothers showed up, begging for food, and Joseph could have refused them or even punished them; but he did not. To be sure, he so dealt with them that they confessed their sins and gave evidence of true repentance; but in the end, Joseph refused to hurt them. He had power over them, but he kept his power under control.

Remember: meekness does not show itself when we are wrong, but when we are right. Meekness is not the shamefaced boy who is caught with his hand in the cookie jar. Meekness is not embarrassment when I am caught doing something wrong. Meekness is power under control. It reveals itself when I am right and when I have the power to hurt somebody who is wrong.

I think of David as another illustration of meekness. David's greatest victories were not with his hands but with his heart. You will recall that in 1 Samuel 24, Saul blundered into the cave where David and his men were hiding, and then went to sleep. With one flashing stroke of his sword, David could have killed Saul and taken the throne. In fact, some of David's men urged him to do just that and put an end to the man who was chasing them and seeking their lives. Instead of cutting off Saul's head, David quietly cut off the skirt of Saul's robe; and even that action made him feel guilty. David had the power to kill Saul, but he kept his power under control.

There is another episode in David's life that reveals his meekness in an even greater measure. It is recorded in 2 Samuel 16. David's son Absalom took over the kingdom and forced his father to flee into the wilderness. During that difficult time, one of Saul's men, Shimei, cursed David and threw stones at him. Abishai, David's nephew, said to the king, "Let me go over, I pray thee, and take off his head" (v. 9). That would have been a reasonable thing to do, but David would not permit it. His only answer was, "Let him alone, and let him curse; for the LORD hath bidden him." That is power under control.

You can be sure that Saul would have killed David had he caught him in the cave; and no doubt Saul would have killed Shimei, too. The difference between these two kings is not that one had power and the other did not, for both had power. The difference is that David's power was under control. He was a meek man. David used his authority to build up people; Saul used people to build up his authority. At one time, Saul was going to kill his own son for a trivial matter, just to show the people how powerful he was (1 Samuel 14:36-45). David was willing to die for his own son, even though Absalom was a rebel (2 Samuel 18:33).

Of course, the greatest example of meekness is our Lord Jesus Christ. "He is brought as a lamb to the slaughter, and as a sheep before her shearers is dumb, so he openeth not his mouth" (Isaiah 53:7). "Who, when he was reviled, reviled not again; when he suffered, he threatened not; but committed himself to him that judgeth righteously" (1 Peter 2:23). It took more power for Jesus to submit than for Peter to draw out his sword and fight. Peter's action was natural; what our Lord did was supernatural. Jesus exercised power under control. He could have summoned legions of angels, but instead he "became obedient unto death, even the death of the cross" (Philippians 2:8).

III

How can you and I tell whether or not we are meek?

Perhaps the simplest answer is a question: are we exercising self-control? Is our power under control? We have physical power, mental power, emotional power, even spiritual power. Are we keeping all of this power under control?

But I think that the best test of meekness is found in the word *attitude*. For example, what is our attitude toward the circumstances of life? When Jesus said, "Blessed are the meek, for they shall inherit the earth," He was quoting from Psalm 37:11, "But the meek shall inherit the earth; and shall delight themselves in the abundance of peace." When you read Psalm 37, you discover that the writer was going through a great deal of trouble. Evil unbelievers were trying to cut him down. They were slandering him and trying to ruin his reputation. In fact, they were plotting against him and trying to take his life! Perhaps you and I have never had our lives threatened, but we have experienced difficult circumstances. How do we respond to them? What is our attitude toward the difficulties of life?

Too many people respond—or react—to the difficulties of life by fretting. "Fret not thyself!" says the opening verse of

Psalm 37, and it is repeated in verse 8: "Cease from anger, and forsake wrath: fret not thyself in any wise to do evil." The normal thing to do when people attack you is to get angry, fret over it, and fight back; but this is not the spiritual thing to do. The meek man submits himself, *and his enemy,* to God and lets God handle the problem. Look at the admonitions in Psalm 37: "Trust in the LORD . . . delight thyself also in the LORD . . . rest in the LORD and wait patiently for Him . . . cease from anger . . . depart from evil and do good." The meek man centers his attention and his affection on *the Lord,* not on himself or his adversary. When you find yourself fretting because of people or circumstances, you can be sure that you have lost your meekness.

Another test of meekness is, what is my attitude toward God's Word? James 1:19 commands us to be "swift to hear, slow to speak, slow to wrath"; and James 1:21 commands us to "receive with meekness the engrafted [implanted] word." James wrote his letter to a group of Christians who were at war with each other! "From whence come wars and fightings among you?" (4:1). One reason for their division was a stubborn attitude toward God's Word. Instead of receiving God's Word with meekness, like planting seed in soft soil, they were arguing with it and becoming angry at it. They were not "slow to speak, slow to wrath." The meek Christian submits to the Word of God and receives it gladly into a prepared heart.

Again we see the contrast between Saul and David. When Samuel gave Saul God's message, the king argued with it and tried to excuse himself. He blamed the people—and he even blamed Samuel! "Because I saw that the people were scattered from me, and that thou camest not within the days appointed, and that the Philistines gathered themselves together" (1 Samuel 13:11). Later, God gave Saul another chance to live like a king, and again he failed. Instead of slaying the enemy as he was commanded (1 Samuel 15), he kept the best for himself and then blamed the people! "But the people took of the spoil . . . to sacrifice unto the LORD thy God in Gilgal" (v. 21).

Saul was not a meek man; he refused to submit to the Word of God.

But David submitted and "received with meekness the engrafted word." David's chaplain, Nathan, took his life in his hands when he confronted the king with his adultery and murder (2 Samuel 12), for David was a backslidden man and could have ordered the prophet to be killed. Nathan told the touching story about the one little ewe lamb that the rich man stole from the poor man, "and David's anger was greatly kindled against the man" (v. 5). Bravely, Nathan said, "Thou art the man"—and waited. Would David's anger be kindled against his prophet? No, because David was a meek man, and he received God's Word without arguing, making excuses, or defending himself. "I have sinned against the LORD!" (v. 13). He was a man after God's own heart.

There is a third test of meekness: what is my attitude toward a brother who sins? Do I receive the news gleefully and start to spread it? Am I pleased that he has sinned, because his fall makes my walk look better? "Brethren, if a man be overtaken in a fault, ye which are spiritual, restore such an one in the spirit of meekness; considering thyself, lest thou also be tempted" (Galatians 6:1). When a Christian brother has fallen into sin, I have the power to hurt him; but meekness is power under control. I also have the power to help him. "Restore such an one." That word *restore* was used by doctors back in Paul's day; it means "to set a broken bone." When a Christian falls into sin, it affects the Body of Christ the way a broken bone affects your physical body, and that Christian must be restored. My first response to a brother's sin ought to be sorrow and pity and then a desire to help him get back into fellowship with God. Shimei threw stones at David when David was at his weakest physically and politically; yet David proved himself to be the stronger man spiritually. Later, when David's throne was restored, Shimei came to beg forgiveness, and David forgave him. He restored him in a spirit of meekness (2 Samuel 19:16-23).

A broken bone is a painful thing, and the setting of it can be an even more painful experience than the breaking of it. A doctor does not use a crowbar and a pipe wrench to set a broken bone! He uses power under control. This is meekness.

A fourth test of meekness is my attitude toward division in the church. "I therefore the prisoner of Lord, beseech you that ye walk worthy of the vocation [calling] wherewith ye are called, with all lowliness and meekness, with longsuffering, forbearing one another in love; endeavouring to keep the unity of the Spirit in the bond of peace" (Ephesians 4:1-3). There are people in every church who are always wanting to take sides and divide God's people.

When I was a boy in the junior department of Sunday school, I remember hearing a teacher say, "Well, there's a business meeting this week, and I'm going to be there loaded for bear!" The next Sunday a number of people were missing from the services, and I discovered that the "hunter" had shot off his gun (and his mouth), and there had been a church split.

The Christian who exercises meekness is not interested in taking sides; he is interested in "being diligent to preserve the unity of the Spirit in the bond of peace" (Ephesians 4:3, NASB). He follows the example of Abraham: "Let there be no strife, I pray thee, between me and thee . . . for we be brethren" (Genesis 13:8).

There is a fifth test of meekness in our lives: what is our attitude toward those people who disagree with us? "And the servant of the Lord must not strive; but be gentle unto all men, apt to teach, patient, in meekness instructing those that oppose themselves; if God peradventure will give them repentance to the acknowledging of the truth" (2 Timothy 2:24-25). It is possible to win arguments and lose friends—and souls!

"There is no arguing with Johnson," said the poet Oliver Goldsmith of Samuel Johnson, England's "czar of literature," "for if his pistol misses fire, he knocks you down with the butt end of it!" Some Christians are like this. "Watch out for Dr. ————," a friend warned me. "He uses a cannon to kill a mosquito!" It is a mark of meekness—and maturity—when we realize that good people disagree and that God can bless people with whom we disagree. Even the person who opposes the Word of God has a better chance of being convinced if we have a meek and gentle spirit. I like Dr. J. W. C. Wand's translation of this passage: "The Lord's servant must not quarrel, but be gentle to all, good at teaching, slow to take offense, one who can reduce his opponents by the mildness of his manners."

Finally, what is my attitude toward the unsaved? "But sanctify the Lord God in your hearts: and be ready always to give an answer to every man that asketh you a reason of the hope that is in you with meekness and fear" (1 Peter 3:15). Peter is warning against arguing with lost souls and using the Bible as a club to beat them down. He is telling us to be witnesses and not prosecuting attorneys! Too often we use high-pressure salesmanship methods in our zeal to win souls, but this is power out of control. Jesus could have overpowered Nicodemus or crushed the woman of Samaria, but instead, He patiently led them into the truth of the Word of God.

IV

How can the believer go about cultivating this grace of meekness? Galatians 5:23 tells us that meekness is not something that we manufacture; it is one of the "fruit of the Spirit." Fruit is not manufactured; fruit must be cultivated. There was a time when Moses, the meekest man on earth, got angry at an enemy and killed him. God had to put Moses on the backside of the desert for forty years, taking care of his father-in-law's sheep, in order to prepare him for his ministry. Alone in the desert, caring for the meekest of animals, Moses began to learn meekness. He was the son of Pharaoh's daughter, educated in all the wisdom of Egypt, and yet he became a shepherd.

We cultivate meekness in the difficult experiences of life.

Think of what Moses had to endure as he led the people of Israel. No sooner was the nation delivered from Egypt than the people began to complain; and they complained for the next forty years, until that generation died. They complained about the way God led them, and about the way God fed them. They rebelled against Moses' authority. They tried to organize a party to return to Egypt. When Moses finally brought them to the border of the Promised Land, they refused to go in! All of his sacrifice and work was for nothing! No, it was not for nothing; for Moses was "growing in grace" and cultivating the wonderful grace of meekness. Moses had always had power, but it was not under control. It was in the school of hard knocks that he learned to be meek.

King Saul never learned meekness because he always tried to scheme his way out of the difficulties of life. Instead of trials bringing out the best in him, they brought out the worst in him. And he always had an excuse ready whenever Samuel showed up. "An excuse," said Billy Sunday, "is the skin of a reason, stuffed with a lie." People who are good at excuses are rarely good at anything else. But David profited from the trials of life and, in spite of his failures (and we all have them), learned how to be meek. Saul tried to use his own authority to make himself great, but David said of God, "Thy gentleness hath made me great" (Psalm 18:35). As David reviewed the trials of his life, he looked back and saw how gentle God had been. Anybody can submit to harshness, but it takes a great man to submit to gentleness. It takes a man whose heart is gentle and whose attitude is that of meekness.

Saul in the Old Testament never did learn meekness, but Saul in the New Testament did. When Paul the apostle was Saul of Tarsus, what power he possessed! And how he used that power to persecute and even to kill! "It is hard for you to kick against the goads," Jesus said to him (Acts 26:14, NASB), suggesting that Saul was like a wild animal that had never been broken. But God broke him, and there came into his life a spirit of meekness.

As a Christian and an apostle, Paul had more power and authority than ever before; but he used that power for the good of others and the glory of God. He had learned meekness. The

situation in the Corinthian church, for example, was enough
to test the patience of Job; yet when you read Paul's Corinthian
letters you see power under control. "What will ye?" he asks
in 1 Corinthians 4:21. "Shall I come unto you with a rod, or in
love, and in the spirit of meekness?" In his second letter he
beseeches them "by the meekness and gentleness of Christ"
(10:1). To the believers in Galatia, Ephesus, and Colosse,
Paul urged the cultivation of meekness; and when he wrote to
the pastors—Timothy and Titus—he reminded them to show
meekness. Like Elijah on Mount Horeb, Paul had learned that
God was not in the wind or the earthquake or the fire but in
"the still, small voice." Power under control.

You and I must make the choice: will we submit in the
difficulties of life and cultivate meekness, or will we rebel and
produce hardness? The fruit of the Spirit is meekness, but it
takes time for the fruit to grow; and the fruit grows best in the
storms of life.

V

From the world's point of view, meekness is the first step
toward failure. Unless you toot your own horn, wave your
own flag, and promote your own goals, you will never get any-
place in today's competitive world. Centuries ago, the Athenian
statesman Pericles described the situation perfectly when he
said, "Fishes in the sea, . . . as men do a-land; the great ones
eat up the little ones."

But from the divine point of view, self-promotion is the fast-
est way to failure. "When thou wast little in thine own sight,"
Samuel said to King Saul, "wast thou not made the head of the
tribes of Israel, and the LORD anointed thee king over Israel?"
(1 Samuel 15:17). When Saul was little, God made him great;
but when Saul made himself great, God made him nothing.
Saul lost his crown.

But David showed a spirit of meekness, so God gave him the
crown. "The Spirit of the LORD came upon David . . . but the
Spirit of the LORD departed from Saul" (1 Samuel 16:13-14).

Because David submitted himself to God, he grew in the trials of life and was prepared by God to sit on the throne and rule Israel. Both David and Jesus, the Son of David, had to suffer and be rejected before they reigned, and the same pattern is duplicated in our lives. We reign in life by resigning our lives. "For whosoever will save his life shall lose it, and whosoever will lose his life for my sake shall find it" (Matthew 16:25).

"Blessed are the meek: for they shall inherit the earth." What does this mean? Does it mean that meek people are prosperous in this world's goods? Apparently not, because Jesus was meek and possessed very little of this world's goods. Does it mean that meek people escape the difficulties of life? I think not, because Moses was meek and yet he faced one difficulty after another. To answer the question, What does it mean to inherit the earth? we must go back to Psalm 37, where the original statement is found.

The conflict in this psalm is between the righteous and the wicked. (Note the repetition of "the wicked" in verses 10, 12, 14, 20-21, 28, 32, 34-35, 38, and 40.) It appears that the wicked are winning and the righteous are losing—"Truth forever on the scaffold, wrong forever on the throne," as James Russell Lowell phrased it.

Well, what can the righteous do in such a dangerous and difficult situation? Fret? No, God says, "Fret not thyself because of evil-doers" (v. 1). Fight? No, because the Lord stands by to protect the righteous and fight their battle for them. "But the salvation of the righteous is of the LORD: he is their strength in the time of trouble" (v. 39).

Then what should the righteous do? *Meekly submit to God's will* by trusting in the Lord (v. 3), delighting in the Lord (v. 4), committing their way unto the Lord (v. 5), and resting in the Lord (v. 7). The result is that they shall "inherit the earth," which simply means that they do not have to be afraid of anybody or anything because God is in control of them and their circumstances. To "inherit the earth" means to reign as king over yourself and your circumstances through the power of the

Holy Spirit. "Yet a little while, and the wicked shall not be; yea, thou shalt diligently consider his place, and it shall not be. But the meek shall inherit the earth; and shall delight themselves in the abundance of peace" (vv. 10-11).

When you are meek, you seek nothing for yourself; and when you seek nothing for yourself, God gives you all things. Saul's self-seeking cost him his crown; but David's submission gave him the kingdom. Something else is true: meekness means power under control, and when you can control yourself, everything belongs to you! If you can reign in peace over the kingdom within you, then God will give you all you need in the kingdom without.

The saddest event in David's life, his sin with Bathsheba, helps to illustrate this principle. Second Samuel 11:1 informs us, "At the time when kings go forth to battle. . . . David tarried still at Jerusalem." He was not living like a king! Not only had he taken off his armor, but he had also taken off his crown. The sad result is recorded in the rest of the chapter: adultery, deceit, murder, sin covered and not confessed. About a year later, Nathan rebuked David for his sins and reminded the king of how much God had given him. "I gave thee thy master's house, and thy master's wives into thy bosom, and gave thee the house of Israel and of Judah; and if that had been too little, I would moreover have given unto thee such and such things" (2 Samuel 12:8). God was simply saying, through Nathan, "David, when you were meek, I gave you blessing after blessing. But when you became proud and disobeyed My Word, you started to lose. It is the meek who inherit, not the proud. If you had remained meek before Me, I would have given you all that you needed and desired and more. But now, I cannot do it."

The meek person owns everything, because he is submitted to the God who made everything and controls everything, and this God is his Father. "For all things are your's; whether Paul, or Apollos, or Cephas, or the world, or life, or death, or things present, or things to come; all are your's; and ye are Christ's;

and Christ is God's" (1 Corinthians 3:21-23). "As having nothing, and yet possessing all things" (2 Corinthians 6:10).

Again, our Lord Jesus Christ is the perfect illustration of this truth. Because He was "meek and lowly in heart," He never worried about the people or the circumstances in the world. You never find Him fretting. Often you find the disciples fretting and even fearing, but never Jesus. He never fretted about the storms, because He knew His Father was in control. In fact, He slept in the storm! He never fretted about food. The disciples asked, "Where can we find enough bread to feed this hungry crowd?" (John 6:5, paraphrase). But Jesus was not worried, because He knew His Father could provide all the bread they needed and more. When the soldiers came to arrest Him, Jesus willingly submitted because He knew His Father was in control. "The cup which my Father hath given me, shall I not drink it?" (John 18:11).

Those who cannot control themselves are never satisfied. There is a restlessness in their hearts that robs them of the joys that are found in the blessings of God. "Thou hast made us for Thyself," said Augustine, "and our hearts are restless until they rest in Thee." "Rest in the LORD," commands Psalm 37:7, and verse 11 promises, "The meek shall inherit the earth." Meekness is the secret of possessing everything! And when you possess everything, you do not have to fret over what others have or what they are doing. King Saul's restlessness was caused by his envy of David, and he literally killed himself chasing David and trying to keep him from getting the crown. Saul's power was not under control, and it destroyed him.

"The meek shall inherit the earth." You inherit something because somebody dies and leaves a bequest to you in his will. In this case, it is *we* who die—die to self—that we might grow in meekness; and as we grow in meekness, we share the rich inheritance that we have in Christ. There is no need for us to assert ourselves to impress others, boast about ourselves, or even defend ourselves, because the Father has all this under His control. The meek person is never envious of others because of what they have. "A little that a righteous man hath is better than the riches of many wicked" (Psalm 37:16). "I have been young, and now am old: yet have I not seen the righteous forsaken, nor his seed begging bread" (Psalm 37:25).

The great enemy of meekness is impatience. This is why the psalmist admonishes us: "Wait on the LORD, and keep his way, and he shall exalt thee to inherit the land" (v. 34). Joseph waited on the Lord, and one day he was exalted and inherited the land. David waited on the Lord and endured the persecution of Saul, and one day God exalted him to inherit the land. The meek person does not fret or fight; he simply submits and waits, knowing that God's timing is perfect. "The trying of your faith worketh patience. But let patience have her perfect work, that ye may be perfect and entire, wanting nothing" (James 1:3-4). Wanting nothing! That means having everything!

"Blessed are the meek: for they shall inherit the earth."

Blessed are they which do hunger and thirst after right-
eousness, for they shall be filled.

Matthew 5:6

As the hart panteth after the water brooks, so panteth my
soul after thee, O God. My soul thirsteth for God, for
the living God: when shall I come and appear before
God?

Psalm 42:1-2

O God, thou art my God; early will I seek thee: my soul
thirsteth for thee, my flesh longeth for thee in a dry and
thirsty land, where no water is.

Psalm 63:1

Ho, every one that thirsteth, come ye to the waters, and
he that hath no money; come ye, buy, and eat; yea, come,
buy wine and milk without money and without price.
Wherefore do ye spend money for that which is not
bread? and your labor for that which satisfieth not? hear-
ken diligently unto me, and eat ye that which is good, and
let your soul delight itself in fatness.

Isaiah 55:1-2

6

The Hungry and Thirsty

FOOD AND WATER are necessities, not luxuries. This was especially true in Palestine in Jesus' day. Both food and water were used carefully and never wasted. The owning of a well and the cultivating of a field were matters of life and death. So, when Jesus linked together hunger and thirst and righteousness, He was telling the people that righteousness is not a luxury, it is a necessity. Our physical life depends upon food and water; our spiritual life depends upon righteousness.

I

The doctors tell us that we are what we eat. This principle is true not only of the body but also of the soul. The outer man depends upon food and water, and the inner man depends upon righteousness. The inner man of the spirit has appetites that must be satisfied, and if they are not satisfied with the spiritual food that God has provided, then they become sickly and weak. If the inner man is to function as he should, he must be fed.

The inner man has a sense of sight. Paul prayed for the Ephesians that the "eyes of [their] understanding might be enlightened" (Ephesians 1:18). Our Lord lamented that His disciples had eyes, but they saw not (Mark 8:18). His counsel to the church at Laodicea was that they anoint their eyes with eyesalve that they might see (Revelation 3:18).

The inner man also has a spiritual sense of hearing. "Who hath ears to hear, let him hear!" Christ's sheep hear His voice and follow Him (John 10:3-4), but they will not follow the voice of a stranger (John 10:5). Immature Christians are "dull of hearing" because they do not exercise their spiritual senses (Hebrews 5:11-14).

There is also a spiritual sense of taste. "O taste and see that the LORD is good!" (Psalm 34:8). "If so be ye have tasted that the Lord is gracious" (1 Peter 2:3). The soul has its hunger and thirst; these desires were built into man at creation. "Thou hast set eternity in their heart" (Ecclesiastes 3:11, ASV). Augustine said it perfectly: "Thou hast made us for Thyself, and our hearts are restless until they rest in Thee." Just as it is normal for the deer to thirst after the water brooks, so it is natural for man to thirst after God. He may not know that his thirst is for God, and he will probably try to satisfy that thirst with a substitute that will leave him with more thirst. But a thirst for God is what it is, just the same. God has put eternity in our hearts, and the temporal cannot satisfy.

The person who has trusted Christ has found the answer to that hidden hunger and thirst in his life; for Jesus Christ is the bread of life, and He alone can satisfy. "I am the bread of life: he that cometh to me shall never hunger; and he that believeth on me shall never thirst" (John 6:35). Jesus told the Samaritan woman at the well, "Whosoever drinketh of this water shall thirst again: but whosoever drinketh of the water that I shall give him shall never thirst" (John 4:13-14).

The presence of hunger and thirst in the life is a good thing. To begin with, hunger and thirst are evidences of life. Dead people have no appetites. The unsaved person has an appetite for sin; he is compared to a dog licking his own vomit and a pig wallowing in the mire (2 Peter 2:22). The Christian is a sheep—a clean animal—that enjoys the green pastures and the still waters. The kind of appetite we have is an indication of the kind of heart we have. The heart of the unbeliever, though it was created with a hunger for God, tries to satisfy itself with "that which is not bread." Jeremiah says it most vividly: "they have forsaken me the fountain of living waters, and hewed them out cisterns, broken cisterns, that can hold no water" (2:13).

The believer who hungers and thirsts after righteousness is giving evidence not only of life but also of health. One of the first symptoms of sickness is loss of appetite, and one of the first signs of regained health after sickness is the return of appetite. When the infection of unconfessed sin is at work in the life of the disobedient Christian, he loses his appetite for spiritual things. He spends his money on that which is not bread, and he feeds on substitutes. But when the Christian confesses his sins and is restored to fellowship, his appetite for the things of God returns.

Were it not for hunger and thirst, we would be unable to live and work. Hunger is a sign that the body needs fuel. If we could continue to live and work without knowing that we needed food and water, we would kill ourselves. Just as pain is a sign that there is something wrong with the body, so hunger and thirst are signs that something is needed by the body. The spiritual meaning is not difficult to see: a hunger and thirst for the things of God is preparation for life and service.

It is tragic when people hunger and thirst for the wrong things. The prodigal son yearned for excitement and popularity, and he found them in the far country. But they did not last, and he soon found himself hungry again; but this time there was nothing to satisfy the hunger. "How many hired servants of my father's have bread enough and to spare" (Luke 15:17). He was so hungry that even bread would have satisfied him! Up till the time the famine hit him, he would have settled for nothing less than the finest luxuries the far country had to offer. First John 2:15-17 warns that our spiritual appetite can never be satisfied by the world—the desires of the flesh, the desires of the eyes, and the pride of life. (It takes a lot to feed an ego!) All of these things are passing away, "but he that doeth the will of God abideth for ever." This reminds us of our Lord's statement to His disciples when they returned to Sychar after going for food: "My meat is to do the will of him that sent me, and to finish his work" (John 4:34). Jesus fed on the will of God; this is what satisfied Him.

What are the hungers in your life? What are the longings that you yearn to have satisfied? If the desires are out of the will of God, to satisfy them means disappointment and judgment. If they are in the will of God, to satisfy them means enjoyment, growth, and fulfillment.

II

Jesus tells us that the way to be satisfied ("filled") is to hunger and thirst after *righteousness*. It is a hunger for holiness that fills the soul and satisfies the appetite of the inner man. It is too bad that we desire lesser things, including lesser blessings. The people of Israel "lusted exceedingly in the wilderness . . . And he gave them their request; but sent leanness into their soul" (Psalm 106:14-15). Had Israel listened to God's Word and cultivated an appetite for His will, God would have "fed them also with the finest of the wheat: and with honey out of the rock" would He have satisfied them (Psalm 81:16).

The theologians tell us that there are three kinds of holiness: imputed, which is justification; imparted, which is sanctification; and eternal, which is glorification. When the sinner trusts Christ, he is declared righteous; this is imputed holiness. As a result of this decision, his life changes, and he shares imparted holiness. The righteousness of Christ becomes a part of his daily life. The person who professes salvation but practices sin is not born of God (1 John 4:1-10). The Christian is not only justified by faith (Romans 5:1), but he is justified unto life (Romans 5:18). Justification is much more than a legal matter recorded on the books of heaven. It is a personal matter that involves a living relationship with God and results in a living revelation of God in our everyday lives.

But what is holiness? To the Pharisees, holiness was conformity to rules; it was an external thing that completely overlooked the needs of the inner man. This explains why Jesus warned, "Except your righteousness shall exceed the righteousness of the scribes and Pharisees, ye shall in no case enter into the kingdom of heaven" (Matthew 5:20). A mere external piety, born of pride and nurtured by the praise of men, is not holiness. If the Beatitudes teach us anything, it is that holiness begins in the heart.

The words *holy* and *whole* belong to the same family. To be holy involves wholeness. Sin divides and destroys, but holiness unites and builds. Holiness is the basic attribute of God: "God is light, and in him is no darkness at all" (1 John 1:5). When you hunger for holiness, you hunger for God. "My soul thirsteth for thee!" And to have God in your life means wholeness; He puts everything together. "Through Him all things are held together" (Colossians 1:17, Williams). When the prodigal son hungered for things and thrills, everything fell apart. When he came to himself and returned to the Father, everything was made whole again. In fact, what he was looking for in the far country *he found right at home.*

To be righteous means to be right—right with God, right with self, and right with others. When you hunger and thirst for God, then you are causing the inner man to function as God made it to function. Your spiritual senses are exercised and developed (Hebrews 5:14). "Exercise thyself rather unto godliness" (1 Timothy 4:7). There is a unity to the life of the person whose deepest desire is to know and please God and to enjoy Him. Instead of running from one substitute to another, seeking inner satisfaction, "All my springs are in thee" (Psalm 87:7). "Lord, to whom shall we go? thou hast the words of eternal life" (John 6:68).

As the inner man is satisfied with holiness, it becomes increasingly dissatisfied with sin. "Ye that love the LORD, hate evil" (Psalm 97:10). To begin with, the mind grows in its recognition of sin. The closer we get to the light, the easier it is to see the defilement. The more we are satisfied with God, the more we are dissatisfied with substitutes, including religious substitutes. The sheep has no taste for garbage! The mind recognizes sin, and the heart is repulsed by sin. The dog returns to his vomit, and the sow wallows in the mire; but the sheep has nothing to do with either one. The mind recognizes sin, the heart is repulsed by sin, and the will refuses sin. It is the appreciation of the excellent that motivates the believer to refuse the cheap and the defiled.

When you control hunger, you control life. Find out what a man's deep appetites are, provide the satisfaction, and you control his life. Dictators and propagandists have followed this principle for centuries. If the appetite is not there, create one. The advertising agencies sell their services for this very purpose. It is unfortunate when our churches create appetites for lesser things—for religious entertainment instead of spiritual food, for multiplied activities instead of spiritual ministries, for sentimental music instead of the spiritual songs of Zion. Having once created the appetite, they must satisfy it; and this plunges our churches into that terrible maelstrom of promotion, celebrities, statistics, and instant results. The sheep need to be led by the quiet waters, but they find themselves drowning in the whirlpool called success.

If a man wants to master a skill, he must have a deep desire to do so, or he will fail. Perhaps his motives are mixed, but if there is a hunger for achievement, he will have an easier time. Change the hunger, and you change the man; control the hunger, and you control the man. Jesus Christ wants to create in us a deep hunger for God, a hunger for holiness. It is this hunger that will change our lives and control our lives as we satisfy it in Jesus Christ.

III

It must have come as a surprise to His listeners when Jesus equated holiness and happiness. He promised that they would be *blessed* if they hungered and thirsted after righteousness. They had seen the Pharisees practice their brand of holiness, and the Pharisees did not seem too happy. There seemed to be no touch of blessing in their lives. The people in that day, like people today, equated holy living with misery! Why did they do this?

For one thing, they had the wrong idea of holiness. They

thought of it in terms of negatives, for this is all that they saw in the Pharisees. The Pharisees were better known for what they were *against* rather than what they were *for.* Unfortunately, some Christians are this way today. Their Christian experience is a painful bondage instead of a glorious liberty. Jesus enjoyed life, even though life for Him was difficult. He was happy because He was holy. The Pharisees were neither happy nor holy, and Jesus pointed this out to them; so they crucified Him. His joyful, holy life so exposed their brittle piety that He became their enemy. Because the Pharisees had a faulty view of holiness, they robbed themselves of happiness.

But they also had a faulty view of sin, and a person with a faulty view of sin will not know how to find the righteousness that satisfies the inner man. Righteousness, for them, was a matter of meeting certain external regulations; and sin was simply not obeying those regulations. They never looked deep within their own hearts and cried out with Paul, "O wretched man that I am! who shall deliver me from the body of this death?" (Romans 7:24). A wrong view of sin and a wrong view of holiness go together. When Isaiah saw the holiness of God, he immediately saw his own sinfulness, and cried out, "Woe is me! for I am undone!" (Isaiah 6:5). The apostle John used to rest upon Jesus' bosom, but when the aged apostle saw the vision of the risen Priest-King, he fell at His feet as though he were dead (Revelation 1:17). The unbeliever cannot understand how the Christian can behold the holiness of God, then confess his own helplessness, and out of this experience find happiness. But, understand it or not, this is the divine formula: holiness, helplessness, happiness.

We must grow in our love for holiness. No doubt, at the beginning of our spiritual walk, we seek righteousness in order to avoid pain, the way a little child obeys so that he might not get a spanking. This is a negative approach to building character, but it is the best way for a child. We have to start somewhere. As we grow in grace, we discover that holy living not only avoids chastening, but it brings positive reward. "No good thing will he withhold from them that walk uprightly" (Psalm 84:11). The danger here, of course, is that we are more concerned with the blessing than the Blesser, and holy living must be the result of a *personal* relationship. When we discover this truth, we graduate into the third level: we seek holiness in order to please the Father. "I do always those things that please him" (John 8:29). The result of this experience is to reach an even higher level: we seek a holy life because we love God and want to glorify Him. The Pharisees loved themselves and sought to glorify themselves, and, as Jesus said, they had their reward.

Seeking to please the Father and cultivating a hunger for holiness brings about a remarkable change in our lives: we become more like Him. After all, we are what we eat; and if our food is to do the will of God, then our lives become the will of God. The will of God is not simply something we do; it is something we are. Holiness becomes to us the beauty of God, and we want that beauty for our own lives. You would never have looked at the Pharisees and yearned to have what they had; but if you had watched Jesus come and go among the people, you would have hungered for what He was. The publicans and sinners were attracted by the holiness of Christ; they were repelled by the religious piety of the Pharisees (Luke 15:1-2).

One of the essential differences between mere outward piety and true holiness is that piety makes you conform to a system, while true holiness conforms you to Christ *and develops your own individuality.* The Pharisees were each like the other; the disciples were individual and distinctive. The more we become like Christ, the more we are liberated to become our best selves. Abraham and Moses were both men of God; yet each was different from the other. Spurgeon and Moody were both men of God, deeply taught in the lessons of God's grace; yet neither was like the other one. The "beauty of holiness" (Psalm 29:2) is not by imitation but by impartation and incarnation. "Christ liveth in me" (Galatians 2:20)!

IV

How does holiness bring happiness?

If knowing God, enjoying God, and becoming like God is our highest desire, then the fulfilling of this desire will bring us the highest happiness. "They shall be filled" is Christ's promise; and that word "filled" carries with it a double meaning: "satisfied," and "controlled by." If we hunger and thirst after God's righteousness, then He will satisfy that hunger; and when He has satisfied it, we will discover that our lives are controlled by His righteousness in all that we do. Seeking to become like Him pleases both us and the Father. The higher we climb by His grace on this highway of holiness, the less satisfied we are with the things that make others happy. The disciples had come a long way in their spiritual walk when they could pray, "Lord, show us the Father, and it is enough for us" (John 14: 8, NASB).

Holiness brings happiness not only by sparing us the pain of sin and its consequences but by purifying our hearts and minds and giving us an appetite for the eternal. "As for me, I will behold thy face in righteousness: I shall be satisfied, when I awake, with thy likeness" (Psalm 17:15). As we become more like Christ, we share more of His joy.

Too many Christians think they can satisfy their hunger for holiness by multiplied activities and special endeavors, when each of these could do more harm than good. It is usually not in the multiplying of activities but in the *simplifying of life* that we experience the deepest satisfaction in Christ. This does not mean that we necessarily do less; rather, it means that what we do is centered in Christ so that He has the preeminence. "This one thing I do" (Philippians 3:13). "Martha, Martha, thou art careful and troubled about many things: but one thing is needful" (Luke 10:41-42). "One thing have I desired of the LORD, that will I seek after; that I may dwell in the house of the LORD all the days of my life, to behold the beauty of the Lord, and to enquire in his temple" (Psalm 27:4).

Growing in holiness simplifies our lives, unifies our lives, and satisfies our lives. No more of the broken cisterns! We are drinking at the pure river of the water of life! No more of the flesh-pots of Egypt: we have the bread of life! The praises of men fall on deaf ears: we want only the approval of God. The wealth of this world means little to us, for we rejoice in the riches of grace in Christ Jesus.

Growing in holiness, however, does not mean that we lose the good things of this world; rather, it means that we receive them back *and enjoy them more.* "He giveth us richly all things to enjoy" (1 Timothy 6:17). Abraham put Isaac on the altar and, in the will of God, died to self; but Abraham received him back to enjoy him in a deeper way than ever before. Jesus enjoyed playing with the children, feasting at the table, watching the birds and the lilies, and doing the everyday tasks of life. True holiness (which is wholeness) touches all of life, not just a part. The Pharisees fasted twice a week and accused Jesus of being a glutton and a drunk. But their fasting was not an exercise in holiness; consequently, their fasting was sin. Our Lord's feasting was in the holy will of God because all of His life was controlled by that will. Holiness always involves *wholeness*— the whole person, the whole of life. "Whether therefore ye eat or drink, or whatsoever ye do, do all to the glory of God" (1 Corinthians 10:31). The Pharisee could never be happy, because he was not whole and his life was not whole. He was trying to patch his old garment with new cloth, and the seams would not hold. Jesus wore the seamless garment of holiness— wholeness—and walked in the joy of the Lord.

There is no holy living apart from the holy Son of God, the holy Word of God, and the Holy Spirit of God; and they go together. The Spirit of God reveals the Son of God through the Word of God. If you have a hunger for holiness, then you will read the Word of God, meditate on it, and make it a vital part of your life. In the Word of God, you will see the Son of God; and when you do, the Spirit of God will transform you so that you become more and more like Him. "But we all, with unveiled face beholding as in a mirror the glory of the Lord, are being transformed into the same image from glory to glory, just as from the Lord, the Spirit" (2 Corinthians 3:18, NASB). Moses did not get a shining face by looking at himself: he spent forty days gazing at the glory of the Lord. Stephen looked away from the hateful faces of men and gazed upon the face of Christ, and his own face radiated the glory of God.

There is no escaping the fact that the men and women of God in the Bible and in church history dared to reject the comfortable piety of their age and abandoned themselves to experience the holiness of God. They hungered and thirsted after righteousness, and God satisfied them. They paid a price, but the reward was worth it. No more could they return to the broken cisterns—even the religious cisterns—once they had drunk deeply of the living waters. The heroes of faith in Hebrews 11 were not persecuted because of their religion but because what they believed so affected the way they behaved that they became a threat to the religious conformists around them. Israel after the Exodus was constantly wanting to go back to Egypt. They forgot the slavery; they only remembered the leeks, the onions, and the garlic! But while they were looking back, Moses was looking ahead; and he "endured, as seeing him who is invisible" (Hebrews 11:27). Moses had a different appetite from that of the people, and therefore he had a different ambition. No wonder holy men and women of God have always been persecuted by the religious crowd and utterly rejected by the people of the world! They had "trial of cruel mockings and scourgings, yea, moreover of bonds and imprisonment: they were stoned, they were sawn asunder, were tempted, were slain with the sword: they wandered about in sheepskins and goatskins; being destitute, afflicted, tormented; (of whom the world was not worthy)" (Hebrews 11:36-38). And all because they hungered and thirsted after righteousness.

If we are to reign in life and live like kings, we must have God's righteousness, imputed and imparted. God's grace reigns in our lives *through righteousness* (Romans 5:21). Jesus

Christ, our High Priest, belongs to the order of Melchisedek— "king of righteousness." The prodigal son became a slave when he rebelled against his father and lived to please himself. When he returned to his father and submitted to righteousness, he experienced grace and began to live like a king.

All of God's blessings are the by-products of His righteousness. "But seek ye first the kingdom of God, and his righteousness; and all these things shall be added unto you" (Matthew 6:33). "All these things"—such as food, clothing, shelter, income, husband, wife. When we live for God's rule and God's righteousness in our lives, then we enjoy everything else!

There is no short-cut to happiness or holiness. We must begin with hunger—a hunger for holiness, a deep desire to be more like Christ. God promises to satisfy this hunger, and it is our responsibility to seek to develop this appetite for the righteousness of God. We are what we eat. "Blessed are they which do hunger and thirst after righteousness: for they shall be filled."

Blessed are the merciful: for they shall obtain mercy.

Matthew 5:7

But the wisdom that is from above is first pure, then peaceable, gentle, and easy to be intreated, full of mercy and good fruits.

James 3:17

He that sheweth mercy, with cheerfulness.

Romans 12:8

Put on therefore, as the elect of God, holy and beloved, bowels of mercies.

Colossians 3:12

Which now of these three, thinkest thou, was neighbour unto him that fell among the thieves? And he said, He that shewed mercy on him.

Luke 10:36-37

7
The Merciful

THE ROMAN WORLD did not admire mercy. The Romans did admire justice, courage, self-control, and wisdom, but not mercy. The philosophers called mercy "a disease of the soul," something to be abhorred and ashamed of if you expected to be a success. Slaves were treated like pieces of used furniture, and the position of women and children was far from ideal. If a woman gave birth to a daughter or a sickly son, the father had the privilege of rejecting the child and having it exposed to die. A temperamental master could, in a fit of anger, maim or even kill a slave. An enemy was an enemy, and the best enemy was a dead enemy.

Jesus Christ and the Gospel began to change all of that. Jesus taught mercy and practiced mercy, and He commanded His followers to show mercy. But when mercy was practiced by Jesus and His followers, it was a revelation of power, not weakness. Instead of being a sickness of the soul, mercy became the very health of their Christian experience.

Our world today is not too far removed spiritually from the Roman world in which Jesus gave the Beatitudes. People are still treated like things, power is the supreme deity, and success is the most important thing in life. How can a person practice mercy in a competitive society? Yet this is exactly what Jesus commands us to do!

I

According to the theologians, God has two kinds of attributes: absolute and relative. The absolute attributes describe what God is like in Himself, totally apart from His creation. God is love even if there are no human beings around to know about it. God is truth, and God is holy. These are essential characteristics of His being. But when man came on the scene, God had to relate these attributes to him; and hence, we have what the theologians call the "relative attributes." Truth becomes faithfulness, holiness becomes justice, and love becomes grace and mercy. Mercy is one of the spiritual bridges that God has built so He can relate to you and me; and mercy is a bridge you and I must build if we are going to relate lovingly to others.

God's mercy and grace grow out of His love. Nobody is saved because God loves him, for God loves the whole world. Sinners are saved because of God's grace and mercy, His love in action. It is easy to remember the difference between grace and mercy. God in His grace gives me what I do not deserve, and in His mercy He does not give me what I do deserve! In one sense, grace is positive, while mercy is negative, although this should not be carried too far. "It is of the LORD's mercies that we are not consumed" (Lamentations 3:22). "The LORD being merciful unto [Lot]" (Genesis 19:16). "Lord, have mercy on my son!" (Matthew 17:15). It is mercy that pities and grace that pardons.

There are several factors involved in this experience of mercy. It begins with pain: somebody hurts us unjustly, and we must respond to this hurt. If we have no power, then all we can do is give in; but if we have the power to retaliate, then we must decide what to do. You cannot show mercy unless you have the power to hurt. Suppose the person deserves to be hurt? Suppose his offense against us is so serious that we feel we must teach him a lesson? We have the power to hurt him back: should we use it? At this point, love enters the picture, not to cancel truth but to control it. We are hurt; we have the power and (we think) the right to hurt the one who hurt us. But because of God's love, we show mercy: we do not give the offender what he deserves. This demands faith; we must leave the offender and his offense in the hands of God. "Dearly beloved, avenge not yourselves" (Romans 12:19). What is the result of this painful experience? Growth! We share in the "fellowship of his sufferings" (Philippians 3:10) and become more like Him.

These, then, are the links in the chain of mercy: pain, power, truth, love, faith, growth. We suffer because of another's sin, but we choose to use our power for growth instead of for retaliation. It is the act of faith that shows mercy that converts pain into spiritual growth. It is love that makes us want to exercise this faith; and it is the Holy Spirit within who gives us this love.

It is an awesome thought that when I show mercy, I am practicing one of the attributes of God. Mercy puts me into the place of God in somebody's life! The Beatitudes begin with a right attitude toward myself—poor in spirit. The next step is a right attitude toward my sin—I mourn. Then, a right attitude toward God's Word—"Blessed are the meek." This creates within me a deep desire for God's righteousness, and He gives it to me when I trust Christ. The first three Beatitudes are preparation for the miracle of the fourth when we, by faith, receive the very righteousness of God. And, having received His righteousness, we then begin *to be like God:* "Blessed are the merciful." "Be ye therefore followers [imitators] of God, as dear children" (Ephesians 5:1). Having received His divine nature, we begin to manifest His divine attributes; and mercy is one of His attributes.

II

Perhaps the best way to understand mercy is to see it in action.

Our first example is in Genesis 14, the story of Abraham's courageous rescue of his nephew, Lot. To begin with, Lot had no business in Sodom. If he had been a spiritually minded man, he would have walked with Abraham and obeyed the Lord. But he decided to move into Sodom; so, when Sodom was attacked by the enemy kings, Lot had to suffer the consequences.

He and his family were taken captive and all their possessions confiscated. When the word got to Abraham, the patriarch immediately gathered his servants and, with the help of God, went out to battle and rescued Lot. This was an act of mercy. Abraham could have said, "Well, the young man is stubborn and didn't know when he was well-off. Let him stew in his own grease!" Had not Abraham given Lot first choice of the land? Had not Lot's choice been a foolish one? Then why rescue him? Because it was the merciful thing to do to a brother (Genesis 14:16). Abraham had the power to hurt Lot, and certainly Lot had hurt Abraham; yet, in faith and love, Abraham chose to show mercy. In the New Testament, Abraham is honored as the great man of faith, and rightly so; but faith plus love equals mercy, and Abraham had all three.

A second example is Joseph. If your brothers treated you the way Joesph's brothers treated him, what would you do to them once they were under your power? They had lied about him, caused him to suffer, and even sold him as a slave! Most of them wanted to kill him! But now the tables were turned: the brothers were bowing before the prime minister of Egypt— Joseph—and he had the power to hurt them. What a temptation! Joseph faced two great temptations in his life, and in both instances, he came out victorious. He was tempted to a sin of the flesh by Potiphar's wife, but he fled from her and kept himself pure. He was tempted to a sin of the spirit by his brothers—he could have taken vengeance upon them—but instead, he went off and wept and then came back and showed mercy. To be sure, Joseph so dealt with his brothers that he was sure their hearts were changed before he openly forgave them; but even this was an evidence of his mercy. Joseph was neither a prodigal son nor an elder brother; he did not yield to either a sin of the flesh or a sin of the spirit. Instead, he was like Jesus Christ, the Son of God, who prayed, "Father, forgive them, for they know not what they do" (Luke 23:34).

Our third example of true mercy is David, the man after God's own heart—and therefore the man who revealed God's own heart. David was the true, anointed king of Israel, even though Saul was still exercising power and using that power to persecute David and his men. On two occasions, David had Saul in his power and could have killed him (1 Samuel 24, 26), but he refused to do so. Instead, he showed mercy. Some of his men wanted David to kill their enemy; they argued that God had brought Saul into their power. But David knew that his real power was not in killing but in showing mercy. Saul had reigned in malice and hatred, but David would reign in love and mercy. In fact, when Saul finally was killed, David sang a lamentation and made no mention whatsoever of Saul's hatred toward him (2 Samuel 1:17-27). "The beauty of Israel is slain upon thy high places: how are the mighty fallen!"

In each of these instances, there was pain and the power to retaliate. But there was also "faith which worketh by love" (Galatians 5:6), and this resulted in mercy. The act of mercy put the one showing mercy on the throne—for it was Abraham who was in control, not Lot; and it was Joseph and David who reigned in life, not their persecutors. We might add that Joseph's experience of mercy made life happier and easier for his brothers, and they reigned in life with him. When you show mercy, it not only helps you to grow and reign, but it also helps others. If, like Saul, they refuse the mercy, then God will judge them. If, like Joseph's brothers, they accept the mercy, God will bless them. The choice is theirs, not ours.

III

The greatest example of showing mercy is seen, of course, in the life of our Lord Jesus Christ. How simple it would have been for Him to answer His enemies with deeds of judgmental power instead of words of grace. The intensity of their opposition increased the closer He got to Calvary, and yet the strength of His mercy matched the intensity of their hatred. Not that He refused to expose their sins: the sermon in Matthew 23 is proof enough that mercy does not sweep the dust under the rug. When the chief priests and rulers had Him arrested, they gave Him in that act a glorious opportunity to avenge Himself. Had He done so, nobody would have criticized Him. Instead, He willingly submitted to the mob and rebuked His impetuous disciple. "Thinkest thou that I cannot now pray to my Father, and he shall presently give me more than twelve legions of angels?" (Matthew 26:53).

We see in Jesus Christ the fulfillment of Psalm 85:10— "Mercy and truth are met together; righteousness and peace have kissed each other." He knew the truth about sinners and even exposed the truth about sinners, and yet He showed mercy to them! The feeble mercy that cultured men show to each other is usually based on ignorance or deception. "If we knew all, we would forgive all," is their motto. Or, "I am just as sinful as you are, so I will show mercy to you because you will show mercy to me." While it is better than nothing, the humanistic approach to mercy is far short of the divine ideal.

Jesus showed mercy, yet He certainly could not plead either ignorance or sin. Jesus "needed not that any should testify of man: for he knew what was in man" (John 2:25). "Which of you convinceth me of sin?" (John 8:46). He was able to show mercy *because of His work on the cross.* It was there that mercy and truth met together and righteousness and peace kissed each other. His death at Calvary was a testimony to the truth that we are sinners, and yet it was also a triumph over sin in that it opened up the fountains of the mercy of God. There is a "judgment without mercy" (James 2:13), but it was not at Calvary. On the cross, there was judgment *with* mercy.

This fact suggests that you and I, if we are not discerning, can practice a kind of counterfeit mercy that denies truth and righteousness and that does not lead to peace. Perhaps this is the kind of mercy that David showed to Absalom when he let him off easy and thus sowed the seeds of rebellion in the boy's heart. David's mourning over Absalom's death is one of the most poignant scenes in all literature, but all the king's horses and all the king's men could never change Absalom's character, let alone his tragic destiny. Whenever mercy is extended, it must be on the basis of truth; and David's mercy toward his son was not on that basis. There is no record that Absalom ever repented (this is where truth comes in) or that David ever encouraged him to repent (this is where righteousness comes in). The whole transaction was shallow and sentimental, not spiritual. We have too many transactions of the same tragic character in our churches today.

Another example of counterfeit mercy is Ahab's treatment of Ben-Hadad (1 Kings 20:32). Ordered to slay the enemy king, Ahab spared him in what seemed to be a great act of mercy. But mercy and truth did not meet that day, and the result was not righteousness or peace. The result was sin and war. Ahab spared his enemy in order to feed his own ego and become a great hero. He gave no thought to the will of God or the glory of God.

To extend mercy means to withhold judgment. Mercy means that God does not give us what we do deserve. But there can be no true mercy apart from justice; somebody simply has to pay the price for sin. This is where the cross comes in: "Who his own self bare our sins in his own body on the tree" (1 Peter 2:24). God forgives us and shows us mercy on the basis of His Son's sacrifice, and we show mercy to others on that same basis. Were it not for Calvary, mercy and truth could never meet together, righteousness and peace would never result.

"Father, forgive them, for they know not what they do" (Luke 23:34). Of what were they ignorant? Of the Person against whom they were sinning, for one thing. "And now, brethren, I [know] that through ignorance ye did it, as did also your rulers" (Acts 3:17). They were also ignorant of the enormity of their sin. They were rejecting God and making God suffer! Ignorance does not remove guilt, but it does mitigate the sentence. Our Lord's prayer for the nation did not automatically result in the personal forgiveness of every man who had been involved in His arrest and crucifixion. But it did postpone God's judgment and give the nation another opportunity to repent. This is mercy.

It is the cross that makes mercy available to us and through us. We must never extend mercy on the basis of our own "spirituality" but rather on the basis of His finished sacrifice. If the mercy we show bypasses the cross, then it also bypasses truth and righteousness, and it can never lead to peace. "But the wisdom that is from above is first pure, then peaceable" (James 3:17). "Peace at any price" is never a basis for mercy. "And having made peace through the blood of his cross" (Colossians 1:20) is the only true basis for mercy. How can we tell the one from the other in actual practice? Counterfeit mercy always inflates the ego of the believer, but true mercy humbles you and gives God the glory.

IV

You cannot extend mercy until you have received mercy. Mercy is not a quality natural to man; it must be received as a gift from God. "Not by works of righteousness which we have done, but according to his mercy he saved us" (Titus 3:5). But the receiving of mercy cannot be a mere commercial transaction between me and God; *I must experience it in my heart.* The problem with the unmerciful servant in Christ's parable (Matthew 18:21-35) was that he looked upon the king's mercy as something that could have been earned if only there had been time enough to work. "Lord, have patience with me, and I will pay thee all!" The man was never really broken by the debt of his sins, and therefore, his attitude was that of a prankster who had gotten off the hook and not of a rebel who had been delivered from death. He received mercy in a commercial way; he did not experience mercy in a spiritual way. For this reason he was unable to extend mercy to his fellow worker, who owed him a paltry sum when compared with his own debt.

The need to experience mercy may help to explain the Lord's Supper. Most of us want to forget the death of a loved one, yet Jesus wants us to remember His death. Why? In coming to the Lord's Supper, we must first examine ourselves (1 Corinthians 11:28), and this means to be confronted with mercy and truth. We must confess the truth about ourselves, and then claim His mercy in forgiveness. We do not come to the Lord's Table to remember our sins; we come to remember Christ. But we cannot eat and drink in a worthy manner if we do not tell the truth to ourselves and to God. The broken bread and the cup remind us of the mercy of God. "And thou shalt remember that thou wast a bondman in the land of Egypt, and the LORD thy God redeemed thee" (Deuteronomy 15:15). The Christian never says with the worldly sentimentalist, "I am a sinner, therefore, I can show mercy to you." Rather, he says "I am a *forgiven* sinner, and because I have experienced mercy and truth at Calvary, I can extend mercy to you." Sins committed can never be the fountain for mercy. It is when sins are *forgiven* that "mercy and truth are met together."

But salvation is but the beginning; there must also be submission. Have you ever noticed that Romans 12 begins with surrender and ends with "Dearly beloved, avenge not yourselves"? Being a "living sacrifice" means *living the sacrifice of Christ*. It was while they were crucifying Him that He repeatedly prayed, "Father forgive them, for they know not what they do." Romans 12 does not stop with verse 2! It goes on to say, "Bless them which persecute you: bless, and curse not. . . . Recompense to no man evil for evil. . . . Dearly beloved, avenge not yourselves. . . . Be not overcome of evil, but overcome evil with good" (Romans 12:14, 17, 19, 21). David knew that it was not his privilege to exercise vengeance, so he left Saul in the hands of God. David showed mercy. Because he was submitted to the will of God, he was able to "give place unto" the wrath of God (Romans 12:19).

Besides salvation and submission, there is a third essential that we must possess if we are going to extend mercy, and that is suffering. When mercy and truth meet together, the result has to be suffering. The one extending mercy suffers because he experiences the hurt caused by his enemy; and the one receiving mercy suffers as he realizes what he has done and repents of his sin. Whenever you are dealing with sin, there is going to be pain. But the experience of mercy heals the wounds and turns the suffering into joy.

This principle is illustrated in John 8, where the Pharisees burst into our Lord's morning message and confronted Him with the woman taken in the very act of adultery. The record indicates that there are several ways to deal with sin. There is the way of Moses, the way of Law. "Now Moses in the law commanded us, that such should be stoned" (John 8:5). Law can never cleanse; it can only condemn. It cannot give power to keep from sinning; it can only inflict judgment after sin has been committed. This way, Jesus rejected.

A second way to deal with sin is man's way: find the sinner, expose the sinner, even use the sinner to accomplish your own selfish purposes. Play God! Jesus dealt with this egotistical approach in one simple sentence: "He that is without sin among you, let him first cast a stone at her" (John 8:7).

If Moses' way is not accepted and if man's way is not accepted, then what is left? The Master's way. "Neither do I condemn thee: go, and sin no more" (John 8:11). Notice that Jesus did not deny the fact of sin. He knew she was a sinner, and she knew that she was a sinner. But mercy and truth met together that morning, and the result was a forgiven sinner. But think of what this cost Jesus! Think of how His holy soul was pained by her sin and by the self-righteous judgment of the religious leaders. And think of the suffering He would endure on the cross to make her cleansing possible! There can be no mercy without suffering, no pardon without pain.

The vindictive, defensive Christian is protecting himself; the merciful Christian is making himself vulnerable. The priest and Levite hurried past the half-dead traveller and saved themselves suffering and danger. (After all, those same robbers might still be around!) But the Good Samaritan made himself vulnerable; he deliberately exposed himself to suffering that he might show mercy to the helpless victim. Expect to suffer as you share God's mercy, for even the Lord could not show mercy and escape suffering. But the suffering we experience is not destructive; it is the "fellowship of his sufferings" (Philippians 3:10). Some of David's greatest psalms came out of his painful experiences with Saul and Absalom. Some of your greatest songs will be born the same way.

V

"Blessed are the merciful: for they shall obtain mercy." What does it mean to obtain mercy? Certainly it does not mean that we *earn* mercy because we *extend* mercy, for such an idea is foreign to Word of God. By its very definition, mercy cannot be earned any more than grace can be earned. The Beatitude is saying: "When you experience mercy, and share mercy, then your heart is in such a condition that you can receive more mercy to share with others." In other words, Jesus is not asking us to be merciful occasionally; He is asking us to be constant channels of mercy. "Give, and it shall be given unto you" (Luke 6:38). By extending mercy, we open our hearts to receive mercy; and having received, we can share again and again.

The Christian is surrounded by mercy. When he looks back, he can say, "Surely goodness and mercy have followed me all the days of my life" (Psalm 23:6). When he looks ahead, he remembers the words of Jude 21—"Looking for the mercy of our Lord Jesus Christ unto eternal life." As he begins each new day, he can say: "It is of the LORD's mercies that we are not consumed, because his compassions fail not. They are new every morning: great is thy faithfulness" (Lamentations 3:22-23).

It is a basic fact of theology that God responds to us on the basis of the condition of the heart. "With the merciful thou wilt shew thyself merciful; with an upright man thou wilt shew thyself upright; with the pure thou wilt shew thyself pure; and with the froward thou wilt shew thyself froward" (Psalm 18:25-26). Jacob was a schemer and a fighter, so God had to wrestle with him and break him before He could bless him. Peter was an impetuous, self-sufficient man, so Jesus had to let him plunge into denial and defeat before He could make him a success. When once we begin to cultivate one of the spiritual graces, *God always provides more.* When we show mercy, He gives mercy; and thus, we have more mercy to show.

When a Christian shows mercy, he experiences liberation. He is set free from grudges that drain the strength and unsettle the mind. The unmerciful servant in the parable (Matthew 18: 21-35) put himself and his family into prison because he could not forgive a friend. The most miserable prison in the world is the prison we make for ourselves when we refuse to show mercy. Our thoughts become shackled, our emotions are chained, the will is almost paralyzed. But when we show mercy, all of these bonds are broken, and we enter into a joyful liberty that frees us to share God's love with others. This blessing of freedom is one way that we receive mercy as we show mercy. It is a blessed by-product of obeying God.

You can be sure that there will always be opportunities to show mercy. We never grow out of this privilege. But what a glorious experience it is! How thrilling it is to go through life sharing God's mercy and not having to judge people to see if they are "worthy" of what we have to offer. We stop looking at the externals and begin to see people through the merciful eyes of Christ. Every Christian we meet is a person in whom Jesus lives; every lost soul we meet is a person for whom Jesus died. In both cases, we have candidates for God's mercy.

The only way God could get His mercy to this world was through His Son. The Son of God had to become flesh before mercy and truth could meet together. It is the same today: mercy in the abstract means nothing—*it must always be incarnate in human flesh.* The evasive lawyer wanted Jesus to discuss the abstract doctrine of "Who is my neighbor?" But Jesus forced him to see one half-dead stranger at the side of the road, and one hated alien who showed mercy to that stranger. The world cannot see mercy apart from the people who experience it and share it.

You and I are to be those people.

Blessed are the pure in heart: for they shall see God.

Matthew 5:8

The light of the body is the eye: if therefore thine eye be single, thy whole body shall be full of light. But if thine eye be evil, thy whole body shall be full of darkness.

Matthew 6:22-23

I beseech thee, shew me thy glory.

Exodus 33:18

No man hath seen God at any time; the only begotten Son, which is in the bosom of the Father, he hath declared him.

John 1:18

O God, thou art my God; early will I seek thee . . . to see thy power and thy glory, so as I have seen thee in the sanctuary.

Psalm 63:1-2

And they shall see his face.

Revelation 22:4

8

The Pure in Heart

AT SOME POINT IN LIFE, each of us must decide what is our highest joy; for the thing that delights us directs us. Generally speaking, a child finds his delight in what he has; a youth in what he does; and an adult in what he is. The first lives for possessions, the second for experiences, and the third for character. We do not condemn the child or the youth for so living, because neither has reached maturity; but we would certainly wonder at an adult who lived on those lower levels. The adult should know that possessions and experiences are empty apart from character. What we *are* determines how much we enjoy of what we *have* and what we *do*.

So, every person has an outlook on life; he is seeking his highest joy. Outlook determines outcome. Abraham lifted up his eyes and saw the stars and became the friend of God by faith. Lot lifted up his eyes and saw Sodom and became the friend of the world. Abraham inherited the city prepared for him by God, the city he had been seeking (Hebrews 11:13-16); but Lot lost everything when Sodom went up in smoke.

If life is to be rich and meaningful, then our joys must be the highest possible; and Jesus tells us that the highest joy possible is to see God.

I

Let's begin with the word *heart*—"Blessed are the pure in heart: for they shall see God." Biblical psychology is not always as scientifically precise as we would like it to be. Paul

109

writes about our "whole spirit and soul and body" (1 Thessalonians 5:23), and the theologians suggest that the spirit is God-consciousness, the soul is self-consciousness, and the body is world-consciousness. Some students further suggest that the soul includes the God-given functions of intellect, emotion, and will. These are convenient categories, but they may not always be consistent. Jesus tells us that the greatest commandment is to love God with all our heart, soul, mind, and strength, indicating *four* functions of personality.

Sometimes the Bible uses the word *heart* to indicate the emotions. "Let not your heart be troubled" (John 14:1). "This is nothing else but sorrow of heart" (Nehemiah 2:2). But the heart can also refer to the intellect. "Why reason ye these things in your hearts?" (Mark 2:8). Hebrews 4:12 states that the Word of God is a "discerner of the thoughts and intents of the heart." The heart also indicates the volitional function, the will. "But Daniel purposed in his heart that he would not defile himself" (Daniel 1:8). Jesus admonished His disciples, "Settle it therefore in your hearts, not to meditate before what ye shall answer" (Luke 21:14).

Putting it all together, you get the impression that *the heart* simply means *the inner man with his many functions.* This is the "master control" area of life. "Keep thy heart with all diligence, for out of it are the issues of life" (Proverbs 4:23). It is here that salvation is experienced: "That if thou shalt confess with thy mouth the Lord Jesus [Jesus as Lord], and shalt believe in thine heart that God hath raised him from the dead, thou shalt be saved" (Romans 10:9). The heart is the center of Christian living: "doing the will of God from the heart" (Ephesians 6:6). The Pharisees tried to please God, but they ignored the heart and majored on outward actions. "This people draweth nigh unto me with their month," said Jesus, "and honoureth me with their lips; but their heart is far from me" (Matthew 15:8).

The heart, of course, is the source of all our trouble. We are prone to blame people and circumstances, and even God, for the wrong things that we do; but the heart is really the culprit. "The heart is deceitful above all things, and desperately wicked: who can know it?" (Jeremiah 17:9). Neither time nor experience has changed the human heart. God's indictment before the Flood is just as valid today: "And God saw that the wickedness of man was great in the earth, and that every imagination of the thoughts of his heart was only evil continually" (Genesis 6:5). Jesus spells it out in greater detail: "For out of the heart proceed evil thoughts, murders, adulteries, fornications, thefts, false witness, blasphemies" (Matthew 15:19). The first step toward seeing God is admitting that my heart is sinful and that I cannot see God unless my heart is changed.

Can the heart be changed? "And I will give them an heart to know me, that I am the LORD" (Jeremiah 24:7). "This is the covenant that I will make with them after those days, saith the Lord, I will put my laws into their hearts, and in their minds will I write them; and their sins and iniquities will I remember no more" (Hebrews 10:16-17). Jesus called this experience being "born again" or "born from above" (John 3:1-7), and Peter described it as becoming "partakers of the divine nature" (2 Peter 1:4). A person is not changed from the outside in; he must be changed from the inside out!

Our two kings, David and Saul, illustrate this truth. When God called Saul, "God gave him another heart" (1 Samuel 10:9), and the beginning of his reign was successful. But then he disobeyed God in failing to wait for Samuel and in acting as the priest; and that was the end of his reign. "But now thy kingdom shall not continue:" Samuel announced, "the Lord hath sought him a man *after his own heart*" (1 Samuel 13:14, italics added). Why? "For man looketh on the outward appearance, but the LORD looketh on the heart" (1 Samuel 16:7). David was that man after God's own heart, not because he was sinless, but because his heart was *single*. Saul was a double-minded man: he tried to fear the people and fear the Lord at the same time, and it could not be done. Saul worried about the outward appearance: "Honour me, I pray thee, before the elders of my people, and before Israel" (1 Samuel 15:30). David sought no honor for himself but only for God. "Let the enemy persecute my soul, and take it," David prays in Psalm 7:5; "yea, let him tread down my life upon the earth, and lay mine honour in the dust." He closes that prayer with his desire that God alone might be glorified: "I will praise the LORD according to his righteousness: and will sing praise to the name of the LORD most high" (Psalm 7:17).

You cannot read the Psalms without learning that David cultivated his heart, the inner man. "I will praise thee, O LORD, with my whole heart" (Psalm 9:1). "Let the words of my mouth, and the meditation of my heart, be acceptable in thy sight, O LORD, my strength, and my redeemer" (Psalm 19:14). "Examine me, O LORD, and prove me; try my reins and my heart" (Psalm 26:2). "When thou saidst, Seek ye my face; my heart said unto thee, Thy face, LORD, will I seek" (Psalm 27:8). "My heart trusted in him, and I am helped" (Psalm 28:7). "My heart is inditing [bubbling up with] a good matter: I speak of the things which I have made touching the king" (Psalm 45:1). (Did not Jesus say, "Out of the abundance of the heart the mouth speaketh" [Matthew 12:34]?) Psalm 57 records David's experiences in the cave when he was hiding from Saul, and twice he stated the desire of his heart: "Be thou exalted, O God, above the heavens; let thy glory be above all the earth" (v. 5, 11).

What was David's secret? "My heart is fixed, O God, my heart is fixed: I will sing and give praise" (Ps 57:7). Saul's heart was not fixed; it was divided and unstable. "A double minded man is unstable in all his ways" (James 1:8). Saul set his heart on receiving honor before the people, and he lost both that and the honor that comes only from God. David set his heart on God and sought to honor Him, and God honored him in a singular way. When the Lord told David that He would build him a house and give him a throne forever (a promise that Messiah would come from David's line), the king was overwhelmed. "What can David speak more to thee for the honour of thy servant? for thou knowest thy servant" (1 Chronicles 17:18). Like a child, David used his own name as he spoke to God: "What can David speak more to thee."

The highest joy of man comes from cultivating the deepest part of man, the heart. When the heart is pure, then the vision is clear, and a man will see God.

II

The word that is translated "pure" has two basic meanings: "clean," and "unmixed." Our English word *cathartic* comes from this Greek word. A cathartic is an agent used by a doctor for the cleansing of the physical system. A psychiatrist also uses catharsis on the emotional level, to "cleanse" the patient of hostilities and other destructive attitudes. There is also a spiritual catharsis, a cleansing of the inner man. "Purifying their hearts by faith" (Acts 15:9) is one example. "The blood of Jesus Christ his Son cleanseth us from all sin" (1 John 1:7) is another.

But the word as it is used in our Beatitude takes the second meaning; for being "pure in heart" involves being *unmixed* as well as being clean. Milk that is pure is not adulterated with water. Gold with the dross removed is pure gold. Wheat with the chaff removed is pure wheat. The basic idea is that of *integrity,* singleness of heart, as opposed to duplicity, a double heart, a divided heart. When God cleanses the sinner and makes him His child, He does more than merely wash away sin. He puts within him a new heart that wants to focus wholly on God. "And I will give them one heart, and one way, that they may fear me for ever" (Jeremiah 32:39). This is spiritual and moral integrity.

It was this integrity that made David a successful king, and it was the lack of this integrity that corrupted and defeated Saul. God rejected Saul from being king, but "He chose David also his servant, and took him from following the sheepfolds. . . . So he [David] fed them according to the integrity of his heart; and guided them by the skilfulness of his hands" (Psalm 78:70,

72). No matter how skillful the hands may be, if the heart is divided, the work will be destroyed. Samuel Johnson states it beautifully: "Integrity without knowledge is weak and useless, and knowledge without integrity is dangerous and dreadful." Peter illustrates the first and Judas the second. Peter loved Jesus Christ and boasted that he would die for him; he had integrity but not knowledge. Judas knew where the Lord was, where He would pray, and what He could do; but he lacked integrity and used his knowledge to destroy himself and others.

Integrity of heart was a passionate concern of David, as is witnessed by many statements in the Psalms. "Judge me, O LORD, according to my righteousness, and according to mine integrity that is in me" (Psalm 7:8). "Let integrity and uprightness preserve me; for I wait on thee" (Psalm 25:21). "Judge me, O LORD; for I have walked in mine integrity. . . . But as for me, I will walk in mine integrity" (Psalm 26:1, 11). "And as for me, thou upholdest me in mine integrity, and settest me before thy face for ever" (Psalm 41:12). That last verse is perhaps the closest thing to our Beatitude that you will find in the Psalms: he had a pure heart, and he saw the face of God.

This singleness of heart is illustrated by Jesus in Matthew 6:19-23, when He talked about the eye. This is in the section of the Sermon on the Mount dealing with our relationship to wealth, and He is warning us against being double-minded, trying to serve both God and money. "The light of the body is the eye: if therefore thine eye be single, thy whole body shall be full of light. But if thine eye be evil, thy whole body shall be full of darkness. If therefore the light that is in thee be darkness, how great is that darkness!" (Matthew 6:22-23). After illustrating this truth by means of the human body, Jesus then illustrates it again by means of human relationships. "No man can serve two masters" (Matthew 6:24). Jesus is speaking here about singleness of devotion, desire, and direction. Psalm 86:11 explains it: "Teach me thy way, O LORD; I will walk in thy truth: unite my heart to fear thy name." No man can ever hope to see God whose heart is divided between the Lord and the world.

Our relationship with God must be based on love. For our hearts to love anything other than God is to commit spiritual adultery. "Ye adulterers and adulteresses, know ye not that the friendship of the world is enmity with God? whosoever therefore will be a friend of the world is the enemy of God" (James 4:4). Because men are at war with God, they are at war with each other. "And Saul became David's enemy continually" (1 Samuel 18:29). The only cure for spiritual adultery is, "Draw nigh to God, and he will draw nigh to you. Cleanse your hands, ye sinners; and purify [make chaste] your hearts, ye double minded" (James 4:8). "Thou shalt love the Lord thy God with *all* thy heart" (Matthew 22:37, italics added). David did not have a *sinless* heart, but he did have a *single* heart; and this made him a man after God's own heart. "I have found David the son of Jesse, a man after mine own heart, which shall fulfill all my will" (Acts 13:22). This verse brings out the contrasts between Saul and David. Saul talked about God's will, but David fulfilled it. Saul wanted his own will, but David wanted God's will. And Saul obeyed only part of God's will, while David fulfilled all of it.

How do we maintain this priceless integrity of heart? *By being utterly honest with God, others, and ourselves; and by seeking to honor God alone.* When you read the life of David, you see a man who sought to live openly and honestly. Twice in his life, David resorted to duplicity, and in both instances he got into trouble. The first occurred when David fled to Gath and tried to escape the sword of Saul by joining the ranks of the enemy. (Gath was originally the home of Goliath, you will recall.) It became clear that David was no safer in Gath than he was in Judah, so "he changed his behaviour before them, and feigned himself mad in their hands, and scrabbled on the doors of the gate, and let his spittle fall down upon his beard" (1 Samuel 21:13). This masquerade enabled David to escape, and one result of this experience was the conviction that faith in God alone is the secret of God's protection. David records this conviction in Psalm 34. Duplicity led David almost to

death. He fled to the Cave of Adullam, and there he wrote
Psalm 57 and cried out: "My heart is fixed, O God, my heart
is fixed!" No more duplicity.

David's second masquerade was following the sin with Bathsheba, when he pretended to honor her husband, Uriah. His
ruse did not work, and he had to resort to outright murder.
Psalm 51 is the record of that experience, and once again the
integrity of the inner man comes to the fore. "Behold, thou
desirest truth in the inward parts" (v. 6). "Create in me a
clean heart, O God; and renew a right [steadfast, established]
spirit within me" (v. 10). Certainly David had sinned against
Bathsheba and Uriah, but when he considered his sin in relationship to the integrity of his heart, he had to pray, "Against
thee, thee only, have I sinned, and done this evil in thy sight"
(v. 4).

Saul's life, however, was one masquerade after another, cli-
maxing in that visit to the witch's cave. "And Saul disguised
himself" announces the historian (1 Samuel 28:8), and from
the human point of view, this was true. But from the spiritual
point of view, Saul did not disguise himself: *he revealed himself.*
In the integrity of his heart, David had fled to a cave and there
found God's help. In the duplicity of his heart, Saul fled to a
cave and discovered that God had forsaken, and the masquerade was all over.

It is instructive to contrast the death of David and the death
of Saul; the one resting confidently and directing the affairs of
his kingdom up to the very end; the other staggering out into
the darkness of defeat and having no control over himself or
his kingdom. Saul's last actions are identified with night: "And
Saul disguised himself, and put on other raiment, and he
went, and two men with him, and they came to the woman by
night. . . . And they rose up, and went away that night" (1 Samuel 28:8, 25). Like Judas centuries later, Saul went out, "and
it was night" (John 13:30). But David's last days are identified with light. "Now these be the last words of David. . . . He
that ruleth over men must be just, ruling in the fear of God.

And he shall be as the light of the morning, when the sun riseth, even a morning without clouds" (2 Samuel 23:1, 3-4).

When you read David's psalms, you realize that he was utterly honest before God. He never prayed anything that he did not mean. If he was afraid or sick or discouraged, he admitted it! Psalm 142 is one of his "cave songs," and in it he says, "I poured out my complaint before him; I showed before him my trouble. When my spirit was overwhelmed within me, then thou knewest my path" (vv. 2-3). Imagine complaining to God! "Attend unto me," David cries in Psalm 55:2, "and hear me: I mourn in my complaint, and make a noise." He was honest with God in his living and in his praying, and this maintained his integrity. He was a man after God's own heart.

The person who, like the Pharisees, pretends to be holy and tries to serve two masters, eventually becomes shallow and hollow. His is a surface religion that never really gets to the heart. He has to use so much energy acting out a part that he has no strength left to live! There is no substitute for integrity. "Blessed are the pure in heart."

III

"For they shall see God." This is the highest blessing possible to man, for when you see God, you see Him who is (as the theologians put it) "the Source, Support, and End of all things." Since nothing is higher than God, then seeing God must be the highest joy that we can experience. It was this joy that motivated and excited men and women in Bible days, and also inspired the great saints of Church history. Moses prayed, "I beseech thee, shew me thy glory" (Exodus 33:18). David wrote his heart's desire in Psalm 42:1-2: "As the hart panteth after the water brooks, so panteth my soul after thee, O God. My soul thirsteth for God, for the living God: when shall I come and appear before God?" Philip said to Jesus, "Show us the Father, and it is enough for us" (John 14:8, NASB). Of course, it was for this purpose that Jesus came, that He might reveal God to us. "He that hath seen me hath seen the Father" (John 14:9).

Why do we seem to have so little of this hunger for God in the church today? We are not lacking in programs or people, activities or "results"; but we are lacking in a vision of God or even a desire for such a vision. The men and women God has used in past days have been characterized by a deep hunger to see God and know Him intimately. They have echoed the prayer of David, "O God, thou art my God; early will I seek thee: my soul thirsteth for thee, my flesh longeth for thee in a dry and thirsty land, where no water is; to see thy power and thy glory, so as I have seen thee in the sanctuary" (Psalm 63: 1-2). If Isaiah's experience is any pattern, it would seem that *seeing* God is a condition for *serving* God. "In the year that king Uzziah died, I saw also the LORD sitting upon a throne, high and lifted up, and his train filled the temple" (Isaiah 6:1). This was also Paul's experience: he saw a light, and then he saw the Lord.

There is a sense, of course, in which God cannot be seen. "No man hath seen God at any time" (John 1:18). Even Moses was unable to look upon God in His very essence. "Thou canst not see my face," the Lord told him, "for there shall no man see me, and live" (Exodus 33:20). Paul, who visited the third heaven, describes God as the One "who only hath immortality, dwelling in the light which no man can approach unto; whom no man hath seen, nor can see" (1 Timothy 6:16). Just as the human eye is blinded, and possibly destroyed, by gazing at the full light of the sun, so the spiritual eye cannot behold God in His fullness. No wonder Moses hid his face at the burning bush, "for he was afraid to look upon God" (Exodus 3:6).

We need that sense of respect today, for too many of God's people evidence a flippant familiarity with God that is not only disrespectful but outright disgusting. They know God in a secondhand way, but they want us to believe they are among his intimates. They have not yet had the deep experience of Job: "I have heard of thee by the hearing of the ear: but now mine eye seeth thee. Wherefore I abhor myself, and repent in dust and ashes" (Job 42:5-6). The apostle John, certainly an intimate friend of Jesus, had a similar experience: "And when I saw him, I fell at his feet as dead" (Revelation 1:17).

No, God in His essence cannot be seen. How, then, do we see God? When the heart is pure, then the eyes are opened to the vision of God wherever He may appear. To be sure, ultimately the children of God will, in heaven, "see his face" (Revelation 22:4). But it is not this final "beatific vision" of the saints and mystics that our Beatitude is talking about. Jesus is promising us the vision of God here and now. It is a basic principle that we see what we love; so, if our hearts are united to fear and love God, then we will see God. We will live in a world that is filled with God!

To begin with, we will see God in His creation. "The heavens declare the glory of God, and the firmament sheweth his handy-work" (Psalm 19:1). The Psalms are filled with expressions of joy and wonder as the writer looked at God's world and saw God Himself. In Psalm 29, for example, David watched a storm as it swept over the mountains; but he did not simply see a storm: *he saw God*. The thunder was the voice of the Lord! The rushing waters were the throne of the Lord! Instead of showing fear as he saw the trees breaking under the wind and the rivers rising, David shouted with confidence, "The LORD sitteth upon the flood; yea, the LORD sitteth King for ever!" (Psalm 29:10). Because David had a pure heart, he saw God in the stars and in the storms, and he enjoyed living in God's world.

Our Lord Jesus had the same vision of God. He saw the providence of God in the fall of the sparrow and the generosity of God in the beauty of the lily. He watched a farmer sow his seed and in that saw the Word of God planted in men's hearts. When the sun came up—and Jesus was an early riser (Mark 1:35)—Jesus beheld the grace of God: "for he maketh his sun to rise on the evil and on the good" (Matthew 5:45). Likewise, the rain reminded Him that the Father "sendeth rain on the just and on the unjust" (Matthew 5:45). For Jesus, nature was alive with—God! Not a nebulous Something—a First Cause or a Prime Mover—but a heavenly Father. "This is my Father's world!"

True, there is sin in it, and with sin come sorrow and death. "For we know that the whole creation groans and suffers the pains of childbirth together until now" (Romans 8:22, NASB). But in spite of what sin has done and what sinners are now doing, this is still God's creation, and His fingerprints and footprints are clearly seen by the saint who has a pure heart. Whenever I become disgusted at the civilization men have built, I look deeply into the creation God has built; I read Psalm 104 and give thanks.

We see God in creation, but we also see God in circumstances. In Psalms 105 and 106, for example, the writer saw the hand of God in the history of His people. Dr. A. T. Pierson used to say, "History is His story," and he was right. When Matthew wrote his gospel, he used the word *fulfilled* at least a dozen times, showing us that the events in the life of Christ were controlled by the hand of God. His birth was the fulfillment of Isaiah 7:14; His flight to Egypt fulfilled Hosea 11:1; His growing up in Nazareth fulfilled the promise in the prophets, "He shall be called a Nazarene" (a rejected one). Our Lord's miracles of healing fulfilled Isaiah 53:4. Over and over in the gospel of Matthew we are told that our Lord's earthly life was a plan from God. And if you and I are in the will of God, if our hearts are single, we too shall see God in the circumstances of life. This was Paul's conviction when he wrote Romans 8:28— "And we know that all things work together for good to them that love God, to them who are the called according to his purpose."

Psalm 23 makes it clear that David saw God in the circumstances of his life. Life was not a series of accidents; it was a series of appointments. The Shepherd was in control. Even when David strayed and circumstances were painful, he still saw the Shepherd restoring him and refreshing him. When

David looked back, he saw God: "Surely goodness and mercy shall follow me all the days of my life"; and when he looked ahead, he saw God: "and I will dwell in the house of the LORD forever" (Psalm 23:6). When he looked around, even when going through the dark valley, David saw God: "For thou art with me." It is significant that in verse 4, David changed from the third person *He* to the second person *thou*.

We see God not only in the circumstances of our own lives but in the march of events in the world. Thoreau was once asked if he wanted to read the newspaper, and he replied that he had read one once! "Blessed are they who never read a newspaper," wrote Thoreau, "for they shall see Nature, and, through her, God." But why sacrifice one for the other? I believe it was John Wesley who said that he read the newspaper to see what God was doing in His world. There is no such thing as "secular" and "sacred" to the person with a pure heart and a single eye. "Who can utter the mighty acts of the LORD?" asks the writer of Psalm 106, whose eye penetrated deep into the mysteries of God's ways in the world. Nature and life are windows through which we should see God, but if we lack that integrity of heart, they become mirrors in which we see only ourselves. Jesus taught this in His parable of the foolish farmer (Luke 12:13-21). In his bumper crops and sudden wealth, this farmer did not see God: he saw only himself. Count the eleven personal pronouns in the farmer's soliloquy, and note the repetition of "I will"! This man was not pure in heart. He did not see God, he saw only himself.

The pure in heart see God in creation and circumstances and also in His Word. Unlike any other Book, the Bible demands preparation of heart if its message is to be understood. As Phillips Brooks puts it, "Obedience is the organ of spiritual knowledge." He finds his basis for this statement in John 7:17, "If any man is willing to do his will, he shall know of the teaching, whether it is of God, or whether I speak from myself" (NASB). We do not understand and then obey: that is instruction. We obey by faith, and then we understand: that is illumination. The double-minded man will never see God in the Bible. He may be book-taught and man-taught, but he will never be God-taught. His mind may grasp facts, but his heart will never lay hold of truths. The Pharisees knew the traditions of the fathers and the opinions of the scholars, but they did not know God. And He was right there in their midst! Bible study is good and important, but Bible knowledge should lead to a deeper knowledge of God. "You search the scriptures, because you think that in them you have eternal life; and it is these that bear witness of me" (John 5:39, NASB).

IV

The experience of seeing God through the eyes of the heart is not a momentary thing; it is constant and growing. "But we all, with unveiled face beholding as in a mirror the glory of the Lord, are being transformed into the same image, from glory to glory, even as by the Spirit of the Lord" (2 Corinthians 3:18, literal translation). The pure in heart have nothing to hide, nothing to defend, nothing to explain. Their faces are unveiled. They advance "from glory to glory" until that day when they see Christ and become eternally like Him.

When you start to see God, you also start to see what God sees. You begin to see yourself in the light of God's glory. Abraham stood and talked with the Lord and called himself "but dust and ashes" (Genesis 18:27). Job saw God and said, "I abhor myself, and repent in dust and ashes" (Job 42:6). Peter fell down at Jesus' knees and said, "Depart from me; for I am a sinful man, O Lord" (Luke 5:8). Paul saw himself as "less than the least of all saints" (Ephesians 3:8) and the chief of sinners (1 Timothy 1:15). The vision of God humbles a man. "Therefore I was left alone, and saw this great vision," wrote Daniel (10:8), "and there remained no strength in me: for my comeliness was turned in me into corruption, and I retained no strength." Spiritual sight leads to spiritual insight. Isaiah saw the Lord and cried, "Woe is me! for I am undone" (Isaiah 6:5).

You not only see yourself in a new light, but you also see others in a new light. When the scribes and Pharisees looked at the publicans and sinners, they saw them as rebels; but Jesus saw them as lost coins, lost sheep, and lost sons. The Pharisees saw God as a Judge to condemn these rebels, but Jesus saw God as a seeking Shepherd and a waiting Father. The Pharisees saw Jesus as a glutton and a drunk, the friend of publicans and sinners. Jesus saw Himself as a Physician who had come to heal the brokenhearted. It is impossible to divorce our vision of God and our insight into ourselves and others. If we would know each other, we must first know God.

The eyes see what the heart loves. If the heart loves God and is single in this devotion, then the eyes will see God whether others see Him or not. And nothing robs the heart of spiritual vision like sin. Saul's repeated disobedience blinded him to God, circumstances, Samuel, and David. Saul treated his enemies like friends and his friends like enemies. No wonder Paul prayed that the "eyes" of our understanding might be enlightened (Ephesians 1:18). Literally, it is "the eyes of your heart." Physically, our eyes tend to deteriorate; but spiritually, our eyes ought to become keener and the vision brighter. If the light enters the body through the eyes, and the "windows of the heart" become soiled, then the light grows dimmer and dimmer. Then we have to pray, with David, "Wash me!" (Psalm 51:7).

The most important part of your life is the part only God sees. He knows whether or not your heart is pure. He wants your heart to be pure, for only then can you see God, and in seeing God receive all that He has and enjoy all that He is.

Blessed are the peacemakers: for they shall be called the children of God.

Matthew 5:9

And the work of righteousness shall be peace; and the effect of righteousness quietness and assurance forever.

Isaiah 32:17

For the wisdom that is from above is first pure, then peaceable, gentle, and easy to be intreated, full of mercy and good fruits, without partiality, and without hypocrisy.

James 3:17

Behold, how good and how pleasant it is for brethren to dwell together in unity!

Psalm 133:1

And let the peace of God rule in your hearts.

Colossians 3:15

But the fruit of the Spirit is love, joy, peace.

Galatians 5:22

9

The Peacemakers

THE BIBLE is a book about peace. There are nearly four hundred references to peace in its pages, either personal peace with God, or peace among men on an individual or a national level. The Bible opens with peace and closes with peace; and the reason there is war in between is because of the opposition of Satan and the disobedience of man. God is not at war with the world, but the world is at war with God.

We must bear in mind that peace, in the Bible, is much more than the absence of war. There is no strife in a cemetery, but one would hardly use a cemetery as an example of peace. In the Bible, peace is a positive force; it signifies the presence of all that is good and wonderful. When two Jews meet each other or part from each other, they say, *"Shalom!* Peace!" but they mean much more than, "May you have no battles!" That word *Shalom* contains in it a desire for all of the goodness that God can give, a total well-being for mind and heart and body. Peace is a creative force, and a peacemaker is a person who releases this creative force to change his world.

If you and I are to be peacemakers in a world filled with strife, then we must understand four basic truths about peace.

I

The first truth is this: the source of peace is God. Six times in the New Testament He is called "the God of peace." He is the God of peace as far as His person is concerned; there are no conflicts in the nature of God. You and I have battles within because we have a higher and a lower nature, but this is not so with God. His person is at perfect peace; His attributes harmoniously dwell together and work together. God is at perfect peace with Himself. This is why He is called the God of peace. One of the great Old Testament names for God is "Jehovah-shalom"—"the Lord is our peace" (Judges 6:24).

Not only is He the God of peace as far as His person and His nature are concerned, but He is the God of peace as far as His will is concerned. "For I know the thoughts that I think toward you, saith the LORD, thoughts of peace, and not of evil, to give you an expected end" (Jeremiah 29:11). God thinks about us; this in itself is a miracle! And the thoughts—the plans—that He thinks are for our peace, to accomplish a perfect purpose for our lives. The enemy would have us believe that God never thinks about us, or that His thoughts are dangerous and painful. But such is not the case. God does think upon us, and His thoughts point to peace.

He is the God of peace in the outworking of His will. Critics tell us that the Old Testament is certainly not a revelation of God, because its pages are filled with war and judgment. But if you read the Old Testament carefully, you discover that God's working is first peace, then war. The account of human history begins with peace, and it is only when man sinned and joined with the enemy that God declared war. But even in His declaration of war there is the message of peace, the promise of the coming Redeemer (Genesis 3:15). The law of war that God gave to Israel in Deuteronomy 20 makes it clear that Israel was to declare peace before it declared war. If the city refused to accept terms of peace, then Israel had to fight.

This same principle was followed by our Lord Jesus Christ, the Prince of Peace. At His birth, the angel announced "peace on earth, good will toward men" (Luke 2:14). There could have been peace on earth, had men received Him; but they said, "We will not have this man to reign over us!" (Luke 19:14).

How did Jesus respond to man's rejection of peace? "Suppose ye that I am come to give peace on earth? I tell you, Nay; but rather division" (Luke 12:51). On that day when He rode into Jerusalem ("city of peace") and fulfilled the Old Testament prophecy, the city still would not receive Him. This is why He wept over the city, saying, "If thou hadst known, even thou, at least in this thy day, the things which belong unto thy peace! But now they are hid from thine eyes" (Luke 19:42). There was certainly no peace on earth!

Was there peace any place? Yes! The whole multitude of disciples rejoiced and praised God, saying, "Blessed be the King that cometh in the name of the Lord: peace in heaven, and glory in the highest" (Luke 19:38). Peace in heaven! There is no peace on earth, but there is peace in heaven—and that peace can be experienced on earth in the hearts of those who will yield to Christ.

Jesus Christ is God's Peacemaker. "For he is our peace," wrote Paul in Ephesians 2:14, referring to Christ's work of uniting believing Jews and Gentiles into one body, the Church. He made peace by His sacrificial death on the cross; and He preaches peace through His Spirit in the world today (Ephesians 2:15, 17). As He faced the tortures of Calvary, Jesus was able to say to His disciples, "Peace I leave with you, my peace I give unto you" (John 14:27). "These things have I spoken unto you, that in me ye might have peace" (John 16:33).

Our God is the God of peace, and our Saviour is the Prince of Peace. The Holy Spirit is the Spirit of peace, for it is He that applies and supplies the peace of God in our lives. "But the fruit of the Spirit is love, joy, peace" (Galatians 5:22). The Source of peace is God, and there is no other source. If you and I are going to be peacemakers, we must know God and draw upon His supply of peace.

II

The enemy of peace is sin. This is the second truth that the believer must lay hold of if he is going to be a peacemaker, otherwise he will misunderstand what happens when people reject his peace. Jesus Christ is the Prince of Peace, yet three times in John's gospel, we are told that there was a division because of Him (7:43; 9:16; 10:19). "He stirreth up the people" was one of the accusations at His trial (Luke 23:5). The apostle Paul was God's ambassador of peace, yet men said of him, "We have found this man a pestilent fellow!" (Acts 24:5). Isaiah 32:17 promises, "The work of righteousness shall be peace," but it seems that those who "hunger and thirst after righteousness" sometimes are the cause of war! "Yea, and all that will live godly in Christ Jesus shall suffer persecution" (2 Timothy 3:12).

According to James 4:1-4, there are three wars going on in our world today.

> From whence come wars and fightings among you? come they not hence, even of your lusts that war in your members? Ye lust, and have not: ye kill, and desire to have, and cannot obtain: ye fight and war, yet ye have not, because ye ask not. Ye ask, and receive not, because ye ask amiss, that ye may consume it upon your lusts. Ye adulterers and adulteresses, know ye not that the friendship of the world is enmity with God? whosoever therefore will be a friend of the world is the enemy of God.

People are at war with each other because they are at war with themselves ("your lusts that war in your members"); and they are at war with themselves because they are at war with God. God has His enemies: the world (v. 4), the flesh (v. 1), and the devil (v. 7); and whoever sides with these enemies declares war on God. Whenever you declare war on God, you become a troublemaker, not a peacemaker.

This helps to explain why so much trouble results when a Christian gets out of the will of God. Abraham tried to escape the famine in Canaan by going to Egypt; and there he created so many problems that the ruler had to ask him to leave (Genesis 12). Lot fell in love with Sodom, and the result was a conflict between him and Abraham (Genesis 13). David committed adultery with Bathsheba and brought tragic discipline down upon both his family and the nation. Jonah disobeyed God and created a storm that almost wrecked the ship and sent an unsaved, pagan crew out into a lost eternity. A believer living in sin is a great troublemaker, because sin is the enemy of peace.

At the same time, a believer living a godly life can be a cause of trouble. Why? Because a peacemaker reveals the war that is going on in the lives of unsaved people. Stephen's calmness as he faced his accusers only incited their hatred the more. "I am for peace: but when I speak, they are for war" (Psalm 120:7). It has often been said that wherever Paul went, the result was either a revival or a riot, and sometimes it was both! "These that have turned the world upside down are come hither also!" (Acts 17:6). As long as men's hearts are sinful, there is going to be war in the world. The only solution is righteousness.

This explains why "Blessed are the pure in heart" precedes "Blessed are the peacemakers." Only the pure in heart can be peacemakers. "And the work of righteousness shall be peace; and the effect of righteousness quietness and assurance forever" (Isaiah 32:17). "But the wisdom that is from above is first pure, then peaceable. . . . And the fruit of righteousness is sown in peace of them that make peace" (James 3:17*a*, 18). If I am at war with God because there is sin in my life, then I cannot be a peacemaker. It was Abraham who made peace, not Lot. Lot was a friend of the world and therefore the enemy of God, while Abraham was a friend of God and therefore the enemy of the world. Abraham sowed peace, and his descendants have been a channel of peace in the world. Lot sowed sin, and his descendants (the Ammonites and the Moabites, Genesis 19: 36-38) were the enemies of Israel throughout history.

God's throne is a righteous throne, and His scepter is a scepter of righteousness. If we are going to reign in life, then we must deal with sin in our lives. Grace reigns "through righteousness" (Romans 5:21). Jesus Christ is "King of Righteousness" (Melchisedek) and "King of Peace" (Salem). In Him, "righteousness and peace have kissed each other" (Psalm 85: 10). David was a man after God's own heart and sought, in spite of his failures, to have a righteous reign in obedience to God. Saul's throne was a throne of deceit and disobedience. Saul's own son, Jonathan, admitted, "My father hath troubled the land" (1 Samuel 14:29). Even after Saul's death "there was a long war between the house of Saul and the house of David" (2 Samuel 3:1) until all the tribes of Israel crowned David their rightful king. These things are an allegory: until Jesus Christ is crowned King in our lives and sin is put to death by the Spirit, we can never be peacemakers.

III

The Source of peace is God, and the enemy of peace is sin. The third truth is: the minister of peace is the Christian. The angels can come and announce "Peace on earth!" but they can never minister as peacemakers, simply because they have never personally experienced the peace of God. We have experienced it, and therefore we can share it. "For we ourselves also were sometimes foolish, disobedient, deceived, serving divers lusts and pleasures, living in malice and envy, hateful, and hating one another" (Titus 3:3). But we came to the cross where Jesus Christ made peace, and there we found forgiveness for our sins. "Therefore being justified by faith, we have peace with God through our Lord Jesus Christ" (Romans 5:1). The war is now over; and because we are no longer at war with God, we are no longer at war with ourselves. The "peace of God, which passeth all understanding" (Philippians 4:7) moves into our hearts and minds, and we are at peace with ourselves. Having received peace with God and having experienced the peace of God, we are now ready to be peacemakers. We are reigning in life because the peace of God is ruling in our hearts (Colossians 3:15).

We begin this ministry of peace by making peace with our brother, and this starts with controlling anger (Matthew 5:21-

26). Hatred in the heart is the equivalent of murder, and it begins with anger. More important than bringing a gift to the altar is getting right with my brother so I can bring my gift with a heart that is right with God. Worship and warfare cannot exist at the same altar. "Agree with thine adversary quickly" (Matthew 5:25) does not suggest cowardice or compromise. Rather, it suggests that we start with the positive before we deal with the negative; it means finding where I *agree* with my brother before I discuss our areas of disagreement. When there is war in my heart, I always look for points of difference; but when there is peace in my heart, I always look for points of agreement.

In the early years of my ministry, whenever anyone approached me with criticism, I usually lit into him and tried to change his mind. Then I learned to agree with my critics quickly, to find someplace where we could stand together, and then from that place move into a constructive discussion of the problem. The words "Yes, I agree with you that—" have a way of disarming people and softening the blow. If you are out to win an argument, you will never agree with your adversary; but if you are out to *win a brother,* you will begin by declaring peace and not war.

Our Lord amplified this matter in Matthew 18:15-17, where He instructs us to visit the estranged brother privately and to seek to win him back. If this fails, then take one or two others with you; and if that fails, it is necessary to take it to the church. The lesson is obvious: the longer a man delays in dealing with sin, the larger the influence of that sin grows. First, the sin involves only two people; then four are involved; and then the whole assembly of believers! "A brother offended is harder to be won than a strong city" (Proverbs 18:19). But Proverbs 16:32 tells us, "He that is slow to anger is better than the mighty; and he that ruleth his spirit than he that taketh a city." If I am reigning in life through Christ and if I have His peace within, then I can storm the city and win the battle in love!

As peacemakers, we are also to seek to bring peace to our

enemies. The instructions in Matthew 5:38-48 are both demanding and disturbing . Certainly our Lord was not giving a set of rules to follow on every occasion; otherwise He was contradicting other admonitions in Scripture. It seems that He was describing *an attitude of heart* that is willing to suffer pain and loss if it will lead to the winning of an enemy. At least this is the interpretation Paul gave to the passage: "Dearly beloved, avenge not yourselves, but rather give place unto wrath: for it is written, Vengeance is mine; I will repay, saith the Lord. Therefore if thine enemy hunger, feed him; if he thirst, give him to drink: for in so doing thou shalt heap coals of fire on his head. Be not overcome of evil, but overcome evil with good" (Romans 12:19-21). Whatever rules my life, I will try to use to rule the lives of others; and, whatever I use to control others will ultimately control me. To be sure, I may not be able to win every brother or convert every enemy. "If if be possible, as much as lieth in you, live peaceably with all men" (Romans 12:18); and sometimes it is not possible. But we must not give up too soon.

As peacemakers, we must never compromise just to bring about peace. "Peace at any price" is never right in the life of the believer. Peace at the expense of honesty and humility will only lead to worse war. The quieting of the surface when the depths are still stormy is no lasting solution to the problem. "They have healed also the hurt of the daughter of my people slightly, saying, Peace, peace; when there is no peace" (Jeremiah 6:14). The false prophets in Ezekiel's day whitewashed the tottering walls and pretended that the situation was in safe hands. "Because, even because they have seduced my people, saying, Peace; and there was no peace; and one built up a wall, and, lo, others daubed it with untempered morter" (Ezekiel 13:10). A false peace is more dangerous than an open war, because it gives the impression that the problems have been solved, when in reality the problems have only been covered over. It is honesty, not hypocrisy, that makes for peace. "But

the wisdom that is from above is first pure, then peaceable"
(James 3:17).

Calvary is the greatest example of making peace. On the
cross, God openly admitted the fact of sin. The horror of sin
was not glossed over when Jesus died for the sins of the world.
Instead of hiding sin, the Lord openly exposed sin. *But then
He suffered for sin.* And because of His sacrifice, we are forgiven and we can be forgiving. We need never fear to deal with
sin, because it has already been dealt with at Calvary. The
cross was His throne, and Jesus reigned as King when He made
peace by the blood of His cross. His scepter had been a reed,
and His crown was made of thorns; but He reigned, just the
same. As believers, we, too, reign in life whenever we honestly
and humbly deal with sin as we seek to win our brother or our
enemy.

There is a price to pay. Is it worth it?

IV

Yes, it is worth it; for *the blessing of peace is godliness:* "they
shall be called the children of God." The Father is the great
Peacemaker; and when you and I become peacemakers, we
become like our Father. Beginning with the fifth Beatitude, the
blessings received are nothing less than attributes of God: merciful, pure in heart, peacemakers. Children are like their parents, and as peacemakers, we become more like the Father in
heaven.

This fact is certainly illustrated in the lives of Saul and
David. As time passed, Saul became more and more of a
troublemaker and David did all he could to bring about peace.
On two occasions, David could have killed Saul; but David
knew that this was not the way to deal with an enemy. In fact,
when David even cut off a part of Saul's robe, his heart "smote
him" (1 Samuel 24:5), so sensitive was he to God's will. When
one of David's men urged him to kill Saul, David replied: "As
the LORD liveth, the LORD shall smite him; or his day shall come

to die; or he shall descend into battle, and perish" (1 Samuel 26:10). David knew that vengeance belonged to God. Because the peace of God controlled David's heart, the power of God controlled David's hand, and he did not use either the sword or the spear to destroy his enemy.

If any man was transformed from a troublemaker into a peacemaker, it was Saul of Tarsus. The very air that he breathed was "threatenings and slaughter" (Acts 9:1)! He knew the Law, but the Law could neither change him nor control him. When he saw Stephen die with glory on his face and a prayer of forgiveness on his lips, Saul never forgot it. Years later, he told that hushed Jewish crowd in the Temple, "And when the blood of thy martyr Stephen was shed, I also was standing by, and consenting unto his death, and kept the raiment of them that slew him" (Acts 22:20). Saul of Tarsus the slave beheld Stephen the king, reigning in life and reigning in death! (The name *Stephen* means "crown.")

But unlike his namesake, Saul admitted his need and one day fell to his face and yielded to Jesus Christ. Here are two Sauls from Benjamin, both of whom fell; yet for King Saul, his fall meant defeat and death, and for Saul of Tarsus it meant victory and life. In the years that followed his conversion, Saul "who is Paul" became a minister of reconciliation, an ambassador of peace, and eventually he paid for his ministry with his life. But it was worth it all! For Paul came to know Christ and became more and more like Him, even though he saw himself as "less than the least of all saints" (Ephesians 3:8) and the chief of sinners (1 Timothy 1:15).

Hatred can never be conquered with hatred. Only love can conquer hatred. And when love declares war on hatred, the battle is always a difficult one. Love is like light and reveals the darkness in hearts. Love challenges the enemy to be a better man, and this often makes the conflict worse, because no man wants to admit that he is less than his enemy. The quiet calmness and pitying love of our Lord when they arrested and tried Him must have infuriated His enemies. The contrast be-

tween their brittle religious piety and His living, loving right-
eousness was too much for them, so they had to destroy Him.
But a peacemaker cannot really be destroyed, because the
Source of peace is God, and God is eternal. Jesus Christ arose
from the dead, and today He shares His peace with all who will
"Kiss the Son" (Psalm 2:12) and trust in Him.

David and Solomon illustrate two aspects of this matter of
peace. David was a man of war, because peace is not purchased
cheaply. Solomon was a man of peace, and under his reign
Israel reached its greatest heights of glory and prosperity. But
Solomon built on the victories his father had won. Jesus Christ
is the Prince of Peace, but He had to fight that awesome battle
against sin by dying on the cross. "Having made peace through
the blood of his cross, by him to reconcile all things unto himself" (Colossians 1:20). Solomon built the Temple because
David won the battles, and in each we see the peace-work of
our Lord Jesus Christ.

As you and I seek to be peacemakers, men will treat us as
they did Jesus. They will misunderstand us and not honestly
seek for the truth. They will criticize us and accuse us. Eventually they will condemn us and crucify us. Hatred blinds,
while love sharpens the vision. Hatred looks for a victim, while
love seeks a victory. The man of war throws stones, and the
peacemaker builds a bridge out of those stones. The man of
war comes with a sword, and the peacemaker disarms him with
love and beats that sword into a ploughshare. The man of war
throws his spear, and the peacemaker beats it into a pruning-
hook. The peacemaker does not avoid the battle; instead, he
transforms the battle into a ministry of reconciliation. How does
he do this? Certainly not in his own strength! "The love of
God is shed abroad in our hearts by the Holy Ghost which is
given unto us" (Romans 5:5). "But the fruit of the Spirit
is . . . peace" (Galatians 5:22).

*Blessed are they which are persecuted for righteousness'
sake: for theirs is the kingdom of heaven. Blessed are ye,
when men shall revile you, and persecute you, and shall
say all manner of evil against you falsely, for my sake.
Rejoice, and be exceeding glad: for great is your reward
in heaven: for so persecuted they the prophets which were
before you.*

Matthew 5:10-12

*Woe unto you, when all men shall speak well of you! for
so did their fathers to the false prophets.*

Luke 6:26

*Beloved, think it not strange concerning the fiery trial
which is to try you, as though some strange thing happened unto you: but rejoice, inasmuch as ye are partakers
of Christ's sufferings; that, when his glory shall be revealed, ye may be glad also with exceeding joy.*

1 Peter 4:12-13

*And they departed from the presence of the council, re-
joicing that they were counted worthy to suffer shame for
his name.*

Acts 5:41

If thou faint in the day of adversity, thy strength is small.

Proverbs 24:10

10

The Persecuted

THERE IS A BRAND of Christianity today that seems very unlike the kind that Jesus spoke about in the gospels and Paul in the epistles. It is an easygoing, popular kind of religion that is acceptable to the world because it involves no conviction and no cross, or at least no cross as Jesus spoke of it. When He told the crowds they had to take up a cross in order to be His disciples, the crowds left Him and then eventually killed Him. The world has no problem accepting and following a religious leader who permits them to stay in their sins; but they will crucify the man who dares to point them to a narrow gate that leads to a narrow way. Even Peter was amazed that following Jesus involved a cross. "Be it far from thee, Lord: this shall not be unto thee" (Matthew 16:22).

I met a Christian friend one day whom I had not seen in several years, and he was sharing with me his experiences as a Christian. "By the way," he remarked, "the last time I heard you preach, you talked about Christians being persecuted. I'll have to confess to you that I don't agree with you. I have never been persecuted for being a Christian, and I don't think it's a necessary part of our Christian life."

We had to part company just then, but had we remained together I would have pointed out to him that *the righteous have always suffered for their faith in one way or another*. It began with Abel being killed by Cain—and Cain was a religious man, by the way. Moses chose "rather to suffer affliction with the people of God" (Hebrews 11:25) than to compromise in Egypt. Jesus Himself told us that the prophets were persecuted, and He warned His disciples that they, too, would be persecuted. The book of Acts and all of Church history since then verify our Lord's prediction. "Yea, and all that will live godly in Christ Jesus shall suffer persecution" (2 Timothy 3:12).

I

The reasons for persecution are not difficult to understand. Jesus names two: we are persecuted "for righteousness' sake" and for His name's sake. We must be careful to distinguish between *persecution* and *punishment.* We are punished by good men for doing evil, and we are persecuted by bad men for doing good. Peter knew the difference: "If ye be reproached for the name of Christ, happy are ye. . . . But let none of you suffer as a murderer, or as a thief, or as an evildoer, or as a busybody in other men's matters. Yet if any man suffer as a Christian, let him not be ashamed; but let him glorify God on this behalf" (1 Peter 4:14-16).

Sad to say, some believers do not know the difference between being offensive and "the offense of the cross" (Galatians 5:11), or between being witnesses and being prosecuting attornies. Jesus used the word "falsely," and it is an important word. If I get into trouble because I talk too much or because I meddle or because I try to force my faith on other people, this is not persecution. If I am promoting my own cause and men reject me, this is not persecution. If I am arrogant and abusive in my attempt to witness for Christ, and people want nothing to do with me, this is not persecution. But if I seek to do His will and honor His name and I suffer, then this is persecution.

Some believers have an ego problem and want to be noticed and praised; so they deliberately get themselves into trouble in order to claim that they have been persecuted for the Lord. The Christian who is devotedly carrying his cross never has to manufacture persecution. If we live the way Jesus lived, then the world will treat us the way it treated Him, and we will share in "the fellowship of his sufferings" (Philippians 3:10).

True persecution comes "for righteousness' sake." It is the result of the believer daring to live the Beatitudes! The world's philosophy is exactly opposite that which Jesus expresses in the Beatitudes, and these opposite viewpoints lead to opposing ways of life. The narrow road that we walk is not parallel to the broad road: it runs right down the middle! We are walking in one direction, and the world is walking in the other, and it is impossible not to collide. Jesus tells us to be "poor in spirit," but the world tells us to build up our ego and be somebody important. Humility is not a virtue that is admired in today's society. In fact, unbelievers look upon humility as a form of weakness. George Bernard Shaw states their position perfectly when he says, "Leave it to the coward to make a religion of his cowardice by preaching humility."

Nor is the world interested in mourning over sin. Unbelievers will quickly regret the uncomfortable effects of sin, but even that passes away. Meekness they consider weakness, for, after all, it is the aggressive man who gets ahead in this world. "Winner take all, and the devil take the hindmost!" The world has no appetite for righteousness. Its motto is, "Eat, drink, and be merry, for tomorrow we die!" Mercy, purity of heart, and peacemaking are concepts that are rarely if ever found in the mind of the unbeliever. To show mercy when your enemy is under your sword's point is to lose the victory. David was a fool not to kill Saul! Such is "the counsel of the ungodly" (Psalm 1:1).

The root meaning of the word *righteousness* is "to divide, to be different." "If ye were of the world, the world would love his own: but because ye are not of the world, but I have chosen you out of the world, therefore the world hateth you" (John 15:19). The holy Son of God was a cause of division when He was in the world, and those who seek to live like him will produce the same consequences. "If they have persecuted me," said Jesus, "they will also persecute you" (John 15:20*b*). Jesus was different, and a world that thrives on conformity cannot tolerate differences. We are children of light, and they are children of darkness. We are alive in the Spirit, and they are dead in sins. We live by faith, and they live by sight. We understand them, but they do not understand us.

We are persecuted "for righteousness' sake" and for His name's sake. "But all these things will they do unto you for my name's sake, because they know not him that sent me" (John 15:21). Our Lord came to earth to reveal God's name to us (John 17:6). Because the world knows not God, they know not His Son, Jesus Christ; and ignorance always breeds suspicion, and suspicion breeds fear. Whatever a person fears, he attacks, and this explains why sinful men killed God's Son and try to kill those who have trusted Him. "For unto you it is given in the behalf of Christ, not only to believe on him, but also to suffer for his sake" (Philippians 1:29). Let a man announce that he belongs to a religious group—be it Baptist, Presbyterian, Lutheran, or what have you—and few people, if anybody, will get upset. But let him announce that he is a Christian, let the name of Christ come into the conversation, and war is declared.

Persecution is a normal part of dedicated Christian living. It is not the thermostat of the Christian life: our love for Christ is that. But it is the thermometer; it helps us measure how much we are like the Saviour.

II

As believers, we must *respond* to persecution and not *react*. We need to be prepared with the right attitude of mind. "Forasmuch then as Christ hath suffered for us in the flesh, arm yourselves likewise with the same mind" (1 Peter 4:1). A proper attitude of mind is a weapon in the battle against Satan. We do not react, then resent, and then retaliate. That is the way the world acts when difficulties come. No, the believer responds in a positive way, not because he seeks persecution but because he expects it and is not surprised when it comes. Jesus tells us that there are three proper responses: we reign (Matthew 5:10), we rejoice (Matthew 5:12), and we release love (Matthew 5:43-48).

"For their's is the kingdom of heaven" simply means that the believer reigns in life in the midst of persecution. He acts like a king, not a slave! The more King Saul persecuted David, the more David reigned in life through faith in God. David knew that he was the rightful king, for God had anointed David and promised him the throne. So he acted like a king! When he could have killed Saul, David exercised self-control and let him go free. When David could have slain Shimei for his stones and slanders, David ignored the man and left the matter with God. When you know you are a king, it is beneath your dignity to retaliate, because that only makes you like other people.

On March 11, 1830, a little British girl was doing her lessons with her tutor, and the lesson that day had to do with the royal family. As she studied the genealogical chart in the book, she became aware of the astounding fact that she was next in line for the throne! At first she wept, and then she looked at her tutor and said, "I will be good!" The fact that little Victoria would one day be queen motivated her to live on a higher level; and the fact that you and I are already kings should motivate us not to retaliate.

After all, there are only three levels on which we can live: the demonic, the human, and the divine. Satan returns evil for good; men return good for good and evil for evil; but God returns good for evil. "He maketh his sun to rise on the evil and on the good, and sendeth rain on the just and on the unjust" (Matthew 5:45). People with low self-esteem quickly react and retaliate, because they must defend themselves. But believers who know they are kings are so filled with God's riches that it is beneath their dignity to retaliate. Jesus could have summoned legions of angels, yet He willingly let sinful men slap Him in the face, spit upon Him, pluck out His beard, mock Him, and then crucify Him.

Our first response is to reign, and our second is to rejoice:

"Rejoice and be exceeding glad" (Matthew 5:12). Impossible? The disciples did it when they were persecuted: "And they departed from the presence of the council, rejoicing that they were counted worthy to suffer shame for his name" (Acts 5: 41). Years later, Peter wrote: "If ye be reproached for the name of Christ, happy are ye" (1 Peter 4:14). How is it possible for suffering people to rejoice? To begin with, we realize that it is a privilege to be persecuted for Jesus' sake. The very persecution is evidence that we are living like Him and glorifying Him, and this ought to make any Christian rejoice. "The fellowship of his sufferings" (Philippians 3:10) is the closest fellowship possible: when we are in the furnace, the Son of God is there with us.

But something else makes us rejoice: we have new opportunities to witness for Christ. Our English word *martyr* is a transliteration of the Greek word that means "witness." Stephen suffered persecution, even unto death, and one result was the conversion of Saul of Tarsus. When the world sees a godly believer rejoice in persecution, it realizes that the Christian life is something more than a mere religion. The greatest opportunities we have for witness come when the stones are flying.

Persecution also gives us an opportunity to grow. When the world praises us, we are in danger; but when the world persecutes us, we can be sure we are living for Christ and becoming more like Him. The furnace of suffering purges out the dross of sin. "For he that hath suffered in the flesh hath ceased from sin; that he no longer should live the rest of his time in the flesh to the lusts of men, but to the will of God" (1 Peter 4:1*b*-2). Persecution has a way of driving us to God; it helps us examine our priorities and strengthen our spiritual roots. Suffering by itself never makes a man grow; but suffering in the will of God and for the glory of God is a great stimulus to spiritual development. "Before I was afflicted I went astray: but now have I kept thy word. . . . It is good for me that I have been afflicted; that I might learn thy statutes" (Psalm 119:67, 71).

This spiritual joy, of course, is not something that we work up: it is the gift of the Holy Spirit: "for the Spirit of glory and of God resteth upon you" (1 Peter 4:14). This joy comes from trusting and loving Christ. "Whom having not seen, ye love; in whom, though now ye see him not, yet believing, ye rejoice with joy unspeakable and full of glory" (1 Peter 1:8). Even our Lord Jesus endured the cross because of "the joy that was set before him" (Hebrews 12:2).

We respond to persecution by reigning, rejoicing, and releasing love. "Love your enemies, bless them that curse you, do good to them that hate you, and pray for them which despitefully use you, and persecute you" (Matthew 5:44). This is the consequence of reigning and rejoicing.

Christian love is not a shallow sentiment; it is a settled attitude of the mind and heart that leads to definite actions of the will. Christian love means that I treat you the way God treats me. This is why Jesus adds to His command to love your enemies, "that ye may be the children of your Father which is in heaven" (Matthew 5:45). God loved us when we were His enemies, and He sent His Son to die for us. We should treat our enemies the way God has treated us—we should be patient, forgiving, and willing to sacrifice for their good, even though they may not deserve it.

If we have sincere Christian love, it will reveal itself in our praying and our acting. We will pray for our enemies that they might come to know the Lord—not so that *our* way will be easier but so that *their* way will be easier. We need the kind of love Jesus showed when He prayed, "Father, forgive them; for they know not what they do" (Luke 23:34). We need the kind of love Stephen showed when he prayed, "Lord Jesus, receive my spirit. . . . Lord, lay not this sin to their charge" (Acts 7:59-60). We do *not* need to pray that fire from heaven will consume our enemies (Luke 9:54-56)!

But it is not enough to love and pray; we must act. By doing something positive for our enemy, we release God's love to touch their lives. This is what Paul meant by "heaping coals of fire upon their head" (Romans 12:17-21). Our motives may be questioned and our ministries rejected, but *for Jesus' sake* we must do good to our enemies if ever they are going to experience the grace of God and become Christians. And even if they do not become Christians, we become better Christians for having done the will of God.

III

There are definite rewards for the believer who suffers persecution in the will of God. Some people may think that rewards are a poor motive for obedience, but Jesus did not think so. To be sure, character is reward enough; but in His grace, Jesus was willing to add something extra. And, after all, whatever rewards we receive only bring greater glory to Him, both here and hereafter.

There is a present reward stated: "for theirs is the kingdom of heaven" (Matthew 5:10). He was not talking about *entering* the Kingdom, because that is covered in the first Beatitude. He was talking about *enjoying* the Kingdom. When you are able to exercise self-control in the midst of persecution, and pray for your persecutors and do good to them, then you have entered into the secrets of the throne and the riches of His glory. No matter how little we may have of material things, we enjoy God's spiritual riches as we reign in life through Jesus Christ. To be sure, there is a future reward, and the Lord names it; but right here and now, we live like kings.

Another reward is our identification with Christ and the prophets: "for so persecuted they the prophets which were before you" (Matthew 5:12). What a holy band of saints to belong to! Here were believers "of whom the world was not worthy" (Hebrews 11:38), and we are privileged to fellowship with them. A man's company is a great revealer of a man's character: "And being let go, they went to their own company" (Acts 4:23). While He was ministering on earth, Jesus was identified with the suffering prophets of old. "Some say that thou art John the Baptist: some, Elias; and others, Jeremias, or one of the prophets" (Matthew 16:14). All three of the men named were persecuted because of their faith and their faithfulness.

Yes, today we can enter into the riches of the Kingdom and the fellowship of the martyrs; but there is also a future reward: "for great is your reward in heaven" (Matthew 5:12). Never minimize the present power of a future reward. Moses turned his back on Egypt and suffered for it because "he had respect unto the recompense of the reward" (Hebrews 11:26). Abraham walked by faith as he looked for that city God had promised him. Jesus encourages us today by promising us heavenly rewards tomorrow, and there is nothing wrong with this encouragement. "If we suffer, we shall also reign with him" (2 Timothy 2:12). One of the repeated themes of 1 Peter is suffering and glory, and Peter wrote to encourage Christians going through fiery trials. It is easy for the comfortable saint to despise promised rewards; but let him go into the fires, and he might change his mind.

IV

This is the last of the Beatitudes, the climax of them all. It is difficult to believe that men would persecute people who are humble and meek, who are seeking after righteousness, who are merciful and trying to make peace. But they do. The dedication of the saints only magnifies the depravity of the sinners.

The world welcomes a compromising Christian but hates the Christian who does the will of God. In some respects, this final Beatitude is the measure of the others. As we are growing in Christian character, we will experience more conflict. It is impossible to have one without the other.

We are never really finished with the Beatitudes, because there are always new discoveries of our own hearts and of God's grace. We grow in grace as we grow in knowledge—knowledge of Christ and knowledge of ourselves. We reign in life, but there is always new territory to conquer and control. We enjoy the Kingdom that we might enlarge the Kingdom, and Jesus dealt with this theme in His statement about salt and light.

Ye are the salt of the earth: but if the salt have lost his savour, wherewith shall it be salted? it is thenceforth good for nothing, but to be cast out, and to be trodden under foot of men.

Ye are the light of the world. A city that is set on a hill cannot be hid.

Neither do men light a candle, and put it under a bushel, but on a candlestick; and it giveth light unto all that are in the house.

Let your light so shine before men, that they may see your good works, and glorify your Father which is in heaven.

Matthew 5:13-16

11

The Salt and the Light

SALT AND LIGHT are commodities that we take for granted, but in the ancient world they were greatly valued. The Roman soldiers were given their salt rations and would revolt if these rations were changed. Our English word *salary* literally means "salt money." The next time you say, "That man is not worth his salt!" you are reminding yourself of the value that people put on salt back in those days.

We flick a switch and have more light than we need; but the Jews that Jesus ministered to had to carry little clay dishes with oil and wicks if they wanted light. When one of our cities experiences a power failure, we wake up to the fact that light is important; but usually we take it for granted.

Jesus used salt and light as pictures of the Christian. No doubt He was describing the disciples particularly, since He changed from the third person in the Beatitudes to the second person in these verses. But to apply these truths only to "Christian workers" would rob us of the blessing and rob the world of the ministry that every believer can perform. In the Beatitudes, our Lord was describing Christian character; and now in these two illustrations, He showed what this character means in everyday life. By using the images of salt and light, He gave us some valuable insights into what it means to be a Christian today.

I

He first gave us an insight into our own salvation. When we trusted Christ, a miracle took place: clay became salt, and

149

darkness became light! We became "partakers of the divine nature" (2 Peter 1:4) so that a new ingredient was added to our lives. Clay became salt! And darkness became light: "For ye were sometimes darkness, but now are ye light in the Lord" (Ephesians 5:8).

Christians are different from unbelievers because Christians possess the very nature of God, having been born into His family. ("God is light" (1 John 1:5), and we are the children of light. Throughout the ancient world, salt was a symbol of purity and faithfulness, and Jesus Christ dared to apply this symbol to those who trust Him. It must have shocked both the disciples and the crowd when Jesus gave them these titles! They could understand a king or a great prophet being called "the salt of the earth" and "the light of the world," but certainly not a group of ordinary laymen. Still, it is true: because of the miracle of God's grace, the Christian is salt and light—a new ingredient has been added, and an old ingredient has been taken away. Sin has been forgiven, the new nature has been implanted, and the Christian stands before the world as God's salt and light.

This means both privilege and responsibility. Along with the dignity of our calling is the duty of our calling. Jesus does not tell us that we should be salt and light: He tells us that we *are* salt and light. We cannot change what we are, but we can waste what we are: the salt can lose its saltiness, and the light can be put under a bushel. This does not deny the miracle that changed us; it only defeats the ministry that challenges us. It would do us good to reflect from time to time on the miracle of our salvation—that clay should become salt and darkness should become light! Taking for granted this miracle of God's grace is certain to lead to spiritual decay. The wonder of it and the glory of it must never leave our hearts. Knowing what I am in Christ enables me, by faith, to do what Christ wants me to do.

The Sermon on the Mount is an impossible enigma to the person who has never experienced this miracle. No matter how religious he may be or how sincere, if he has never been transformed by God's power, he can never live the transformed life described in this Sermon. It requires a miracle.

II

These two images also give us insight into our world. If the Christian is salt, then he is living in a *decaying* world; and if he is light, he is living in a *dark* world.

Jesus harbored no illusions about this world. To be sure, He saw His Father's creation and rejoiced in it—the lilies of the field, the sparrows, even the seeds in the sower's bag. Nowhere does the Bible condemn God's creation, in spite of the fact that creation is groaning because of sin. The heavens still declare the glory of God, and the earth reveals His handiwork (Psalm 19:1). The world of creation is here for us to enjoy.

Nor did our Lord condemn the world of humanity. "For God so loved the world that he gave his only begotten Son" (John 3:16). Sin has done terrible damage to the creature that God made in His image; but God still loves man and wants to save him. The world of creation and the world of humanity have both been ravaged by sin, but both can share in redemption. Mankind apart from Christ is lost, and Jesus came to save the lost.

It is the world that man has made that is decaying, that whole system that denies God and exalts man. When Jesus said, "They are not of the world, even as I am not of the world" (John 17:16), it was this system that He was referring to. We are in the world physically, but not of the world spiritually. Like a scuba diver in the ocean, the believer is out of his element in this present world system because his citizenship is in heaven. The world is a vast graveyard spiritually, and Christians are the only people who are really alive! Jesus looked upon the world as a decaying corpse when He said, "Wheresoever the body is, thither will the eagles be gathered together" (Luke 17:37). And Peter described this world system as "a dark place" (2 Peter 1:19). The word translated "dark" means "squalid, murky," which hardly pictures this world as a paradise.

Decay, of course, is caused by death. When a living creature dies, it can no longer support its cell structure, so the body begins to decompose. When God created the world and the first man and woman, everything pulsated with life. When sin invaded, death entered the scene, and with death came decay. From a physical point of view, decay is a blessing, because it removes unwanted dead matter and turns it into useful soil; but from a spiritual point of view, decay is disaster. It is evidence of spiritual death: mankind is separated from God.

We see decay in every area of life. Centuries ago, the prophet Daniel saw the meaning of the image and revealed the fact that the political world would decay—from gold to silver, to brass, and then to iron and clay. History started with clay, and it will end with clay. Certainly the religious world is decaying: men have "a form of godliness" but there is no power (2 Timothy 3:5). "Nevertheless when the Son of man cometh, shall he find faith on the earth?" (Luke 18:8). One does not have to make a survey to learn that moral standards have decayed. The "perilous times" that Paul warned about are certainly here (2 Timothy 3:1-5).

When things decay, they fall apart, and we are seeing society fall apart around us. Marriages have a hard time staying together, and families are being scattered. Law and order are laughed at, and the basic institutions of society are threatened with extinction. On the outside, some of the structures look sound; but inside they are rotting away, and it is only a matter of time before they fall. The corpse is rotting away, and the eagles are gathering together.

Not only is it a decaying world, but it is a dark world, in spite of the fact that we claim to be enlightened. There is a great deal of knowledge and very little wisdom. Intellectual darkness pervades our educational systems because God has been asked to leave. "Because that, when they knew God, they glorified him not as God, neither were thankful; but became vain in their imaginations, and their foolish heart was darkened" (Romans 1:21). History is not an account of evolution, with man climbing higher; it is a sad tale of devolution, with man turning his back on the heights and plunging to the depths. Man is not looking for the light; he has rejected the light and is walking in the shadows into deeper and deeper darkness. Man's very light is darkness! "If therefore the light that is in thee be darkness, how great is that darkness!" (Matthew 6:23).

Darkness and decay go together. Because there is political darkness ("We will not have this man to reign over us!"), the governments of the world are decaying. Because there is religious darkness, the religions of the world are falling apart and desperately trying to save themselves by joining together. And because there is moral darkness, it is not safe to walk the streets even in the daytime. "For behold, the darkness shall cover the earth, and gross darkness the people" (Isaiah 60:2).

This darkness and decay help to explain why people are confused. Nothing looks right in the dark. You can see shapes, but not sizes and appearances. Everything is distorted in the dark. Is it any wonder that values are twisted and distorted with the world so shrouded in darkness? Gold is more important than goodness, and things are more important than people; and God is not important at all. No wonder people stumble and fall! No wonder men cannot tell their friends from their enemies! When Jesus Christ was on earth, the Light was shining. "As long as I am in the world, I am the light of the world" (John 9:5). He warned them: "Yet a little while is the light with you. Walk while ye have the light, lest darkness come upon you: for he that walketh in darkness knoweth not whither he goeth" (John 12:35).

Is there any hope for a dark, decaying world?

III

The third insight that our Lord gave us is into our own position and ministry in this world. The world is decaying: Christians are salt. The world is dark: Christians are light.

Salt, of course, hinders corruption. The fact that the world is decaying should not encourage the Christian to isolate and insulate himself, or to stand on the sidelines and wait for the great collapse. The contrast between Jonah and Jesus illustrates the point: Jonah sat outside the city and hoped that judgment would fall, while Jesus looked upon the city and wept over it because judgment was inevitable. Sometimes we Christians not only hate sin, but we hate sinners! Abraham knew how corrupt Sodom was, yet he prayed that the city might be spared. Paul knew how blind Israel was, yet he was willing to be accursed that they might be saved. Joseph in Egypt and Daniel in Babylon both acted as divine salt in the midst of a corrupt society, and God used them. Their ministries did not prevent the ultimate collapse of the nations, but these men did stand for God and leave the nations without excuse.

If the world is as corrupt as it is with Christians present in it, what will civilization be like when the Christians are gone? Little does the world system realize that it is the presence of God's people that prevents that final collapse and that ultimate judgment. Lot was anything but a dedicated believer, yet his presence in Sodom made it impossible for God to judge the city. His presence in Zoar spared the city; his absence from Sodom condemned the city. One day God will judge this present world system, but He must call His own out of it before that judgment can fall. Meanwhile, our responsibility is to exert all the power we can to prevent decay and to win people to Christ. This does not mean that we must live like the world in order to influence the world. Abraham, separated from Sodom, actually had more influence on the city than did Lot, who was living in Sodom. And he did the city more good! When the kings captured Lot and the rest of the citizens, it was Abraham who rescued them. By risking his life to save them, Abraham gave them more witness in one night than Lot had given them in years. And when Abraham refused to accept the offer of the king of Sodom, he witnessed to the whole city that his faith was in the true God. Lot, immersed in the activities of the sinful city, had no influence upon his own family; yet Abraham, the friend of God, exerted a powerful influence as he interceded for the lost.

Salt not only hinders corruption but it also seasons whatever it touches. The world is a better place for the presence of Christians, whether the world admits it or not. If we were to take out of civilization the influence of Christian thought and Christian people, very little would be left. This is not to say that only Christians have made lasting contributions to society, because many unbelievers have contributed much that is of value. But it is because of the fruits of the Christian message that mankind has the freedom and the dignity to pursue truth. Even modern science, which may scoff at the Gospel, is a result of the Gospel. When God gave man dominion, He gave him His mandate to search and discover and invent. The furniture of the house of civilization comes from many different hands, but the foundation was laid by God.

When salt touches an open wound, it stings. Christians are not honey to soothe a sinful world; we are salt to convict it. The presence of the Holy Spirit in the Church, witnessing through the Word, convicts the world "of sin, and of righteousness, and of judgment" (John 16:8). This is one reason why the world hates us. "If I had not come and spoken unto them, they had not had sin: but now they have no cloke for their sin" (John 15:22).

Salt makes people thirsty. If we are truly the salt of the earth, people will see in us what they are seeking for themselves, and will want to get hold of it. Jesus attracted all kinds of needy people, and so should the dedicated Christian. The lost may not agree with our theology or even our way of life, but they will see in us qualities they lack themselves and would like to possess. The Pharisees repelled the publicans and sinners, but Jesus attracted them. He made them thirsty for what He alone could give. The more we are like Him, the more sinners will be attracted by our life and witness as we are the salt of the earth.

But we are also the light of the world. Jesus defined this light as "good works." As salt, we must have the kind of character that penetrates and purifies, and as light, we must have the kind of conduct that points to God. We like to think of these good works as religious works, but Jesus did not so define . them. Good works are simply works motivated by love, energized by the Spirit, and done to the glory of God. "For it is God which worketh in you, both to will and to do of his good pleasure" (Philippians 2:13). Unsaved people certainly can perform good deeds, but these are not like the Spirit-directed good works that come from the lives of God's people. Too often, good deeds point to the doer; but the good works Jesus talked about point to God.

Once again, we must avoid extremes. There are those who feel they have not served God unless they have preached a sermon or given out a piece of Christian literature. There are others who reject that kind of service and think only of the "practical" things of life such as healing the sick and feeding the hungry. Social action sometimes replaces evangelism. Actually, our good works glorify God only if they begin with God and are empowered by His Spirit. Jesus said of the Holy Spirit, "He shall glorify me" (John 16:14). Whether we are giving a neighbor a ride to the store, helping a child with his lessons, or teaching a Sunday school class, if our works are motivated by love and empowered by the Spirit, they will point others to God. There are no such categories as religious works and secular works, for the Christian is to "do all to the glory of God" (1 Corinthians 10:31). The missionary doctor heals the body that he might demonstrate God's love and eventually have the privilege of healing the soul. The Christian neighbor helps those around him, not simply to win the right to be heard, but because showing Christian love is in itself a ministry to the glory of God.

Salt and light balance each other. Salt is hidden: it works secretly and slowly. Light is seen: it works openly and quickly. The influence of Christian character is quiet and penetrating.

The influence of Christian conduct is obvious and attracting. The two go together and reinforce each other. Conduct without character is hypocrisy; character without conduct is disobedience. A church officer once told me, "I don't go around the shop doing a lot of good works. I just let my light shine for the Lord." But the way to let your light shine is to do good works! And those good works must be backed up with true character, the kind that is described in the Beatitudes.

Both salt and light must make contact if they are to do any good. Salt in the container can never have any influence, nor can a light hidden under a bushel. Too many Christians have the idea that they are serving God by sitting in church, when the greatest needs are outside the church building. We fellowship with God's people that we might receive the grace needed to serve Christ out in the world. Worship builds character, and character leads to conduct. Separation from sin does not mean isolation from sinners. The salt must make contact if it is to do any good, and the light must be seen. Why is it that so few believers dare to make this contact? The answer to that question leads us to the fourth insight Jesus gave us.

IV

Our Lord gave us insight into the dangers that are involved when you and I attempt to be salt and light in this world. There is, first of all, the danger that the salt might lose its saltiness and become good for nothing. Our modern salt would not lose its flavor, because it is highly refined; but back in Jesus' day, salt did lose its flavor. William Thompson, in his classic work *The Land and the Book,* tells about a merchant who rented several houses in which he stored salt. The merchant, however, forgot to cover the dirt floors of the houses and simply unloaded the salt directly on the earth. When he returned many days later, he discovered that his salt had lost its flavor from being next to the ground. The entire supply was actually thrown into the street, where men walked upon it.

The Christian is not yet perfect; there is still that old nature within that can cause him to sin. The greatest problem we face in serving Christ is having contact with sinners without being contaminated by sinners. Jesus Christ was the friend of publicans and sinners, yet He was "holy, harmless, undefiled, separate from sinners" (Hebrews 7:26). There was contact without contamination; there was true separation without insulation or isolation. Only the Spirit of God can keep us from losing our flavor as we seek to minister to the lost. Of course, this loss of flavor would be a gradual thing. First there is friendship with the world (James 4:4), and then we are "spotted by the world" (James 1:27). This leads to a love for the world (1 John 2:15) and then conformity to the world (Romans 12:2). The salt has lost its flavor and is good for nothing.

We must also beware of the light being hidden. Only we can hide our lights. The religious leaders tried to hide the lights of the apostles, but the more the lights were threatened, the brighter they blazed. The history of the Church is the story of the light shining in the darkness and the darkness trying to put it out (John 1:5). Our Lord was not talking about a person losing his salvation, because such an experience is not possible. His subject was witnessing, glorifying God by the lives that we live. Unless the wick of witness is fed by the oil of the Holy Spirit, the light will go out. "But ye shall receive power, when the Holy Ghost is come upon you, and ye shall be witnesses unto me" (Acts 1:8, literal translation).

It is worth noting that Jesus put the lamp on the lampstand ("candlestick") where it could give light "to all the house." If our light is going to shine at all, it will shine first at home. The man out of whom Jesus cast the legion of demons wanted to go with the Lord and serve Him, but Jesus told him: "Go home to thy friends, and tell them how great things the Lord hath done for thee, and hath had compassion on thee" (Mark 5:19). We think that the greatest darkness is the farthest away, when it may be right at home. And the light that shines brightly at home will reach people away from home.

In these days of mass movements and great organizations, we tend to belittle the witness of one person. "What can a little salt do to influence a whole world?" we ask. "What good is a little candle when the world is so dark?" And yet the emphasis in the Bible is on the work and witness of *one person*. When human history was at its darkest after the Flood, God called one man, Abraham, and this one man has blessed the whole world. When Israel was experiencing its darkest hour in Egypt, God called one man, Moses, and the result was freedom. God has always had His man waiting in the wings when it seemed impossible for the drama of history to finish on a note of victory.

God is still looking for people who will be salt and light. It is a difficult and dangerous ministry, but it is an essential ministry. Salt and light must give of themselves that others might be helped, and what they do is usually taken for granted. But whether or not the salt and light are noticed is really unimportant. The important thing is that men glorify God.